Advance Praise for

The Art of True Relations

This wonderful book both enacts and recalls dialogue as the most fundamental means of human growth. Sarah Wider and Daisaku Ikeda celebrate the self-reliance of Ralph Waldo Emerson, with special attention to the women of Transcendentalism who were mentors, friends, and teachers of new spiritual awareness. At the same time, these two conversationalists reflect on the importance of parents and teachers in their personal lives, and their scope expands to East-West dialogue and present possibilities of fostering peace. All of this makes *The Art of True Relations* a delight to read.
—Phyllis Cole, Professor of English, Women's Studies, and American Studies, Penn State Brandywine

Following the gentle flow of Ikeda's and Wider's conversations, we enter a heart-warming intimacy with them and with their mentors, Josei Toda and Ralph Waldo Emerson. The authors' unabashed expressions of appreciation for mothers everywhere, for circles of support, and for the natural world evoke radical gratitude.
—Ann Diller, Professor Emerita, Philosophy of Education, University of New Hampshire

The Art of True Relations is a carefully crafted, beautifully organized, and deeply hospitable book. To read it is to feel like one is eavesdropping on a conversation between two wise old companions. Throughout, Wider and Ikeda ask a number of familiar but penetrating questions, including: What is the best way to raise our children? How can we engage meaningfully with our work? Why is it important to honor our promises, great and small? What is true happiness? What would it mean to become a society based on sharing and collaboration rather than acquisition and competition?

Their dialogue is far-reaching, touching upon the works of artists, novelists, philosophers, and many others. They celebrate a global culture of letters that draws from Eastern and Western traditions, providing thereby a commentary on the power of such great thinkers as Romain Rolland, Victor Hugo, Leo Tolstoy, Walt Whitman, Leonardo da Vinci, Marie Curie, Alisher Navoi, Rabindranath Tagore, and Margaret Fuller to communicate fundamental and profound perceptions that we all share. Wider's and Ikeda's dialogue is infused with the same poetic spirit that they see animating this global culture of letters.

Additionally, the authors regard Ralph Waldo Emerson as a particularly special muse, precisely because his thinking eloquently transcends time, geography, and culture. Wider and Ikeda reflect on the echoes of Emerson's thought in Buddhist teachings and vice versa as they discuss mutual commitments to anti-discrimination, human potential, world peace, and the beautiful dignity of true relations.

I strongly recommend this book to anyone interested in living more humanely. It should serve as an invaluable resource for humanistically inclined educators everywhere.

—Megan Laverty, Associate Professor of Philosophy and Education at Teachers College, Columbia University

The Art of True Relations

The Art of True Relations

Conversations on the Poetic Heart of Human Possibility

SARAH WIDER

DAISAKU IKEDA

Dialogue Path Press
Cambridge, Massachusetts
2014

Published by Dialogue Path Press
Ikeda Center for Peace, Learning, and Dialogue
396 Harvard Street
Cambridge, Massachusetts 02138

Cover design by Gopa & Ted2, Inc.
Interior design by Gopa & Ted2, Inc., and Eric Edstam
Cover image copyright © The Metropolitan Museum of Art.
Pieced Quilt. 1930. Made by Y. L. Amish, Indiana. Wool
and cotton, 84 x 71 in. (213.4 x 180.3 cm). Friends of the
American Wing Fund, 1988 (1988.128). The cover image
is a detail. For full image, see last page.

ISBN: 978-1-887917-11-7

Library of Congress Cataloging-in-Publication Data

Wider, Sarah Ann.
The art of true relations : conversations on the poetic heart of human
possibility / Sarah Ann Wider, Daisaku Ikeda. — One [edition].
    pages cm
Includes bibliographical references and index.
ISBN 978-1-887917-11-7 (alk. paper)
1. Transcendentalism. 2. Philosophy, Modern. 3. Humanism. I. Title.
B823.W53 2014
141'.3—dc23

                                        2013041655

10 9 8 7 6 5 4 3 2 1

About Dialogue Path Press

Dialogue Path Press is the publishing arm of the Ikeda Center for Peace, Learning, and Dialogue, and is dedicated to publishing titles that foster cross-cultural dialogue and greater human flourishing. Books published by the Center (including those produced in collaboration with other publishers) have been used in more than 800 college and university courses. Previous Dialogue Path Press titles are:

America Will Be!: Conversations on Hope, Freedom, and Democracy (2013)

The Inner Philosopher: Conversations on Philosophy's Transformative Power (2012)

Into Full Flower: Making Peace Cultures Happen (2010)

Creating Waldens: An East-West Conversation on the American Renaissance (2009)

About the Ikeda Center

The Ikeda Center for Peace, Learning, and Dialogue is a not-for-profit institution founded by Buddhist thinker and leader Daisaku Ikeda in 1993. Located in Cambridge, Massachusetts, the Center engages diverse scholars, activists, and social innovators in the search for the ideas and solutions that will assist in the peaceful evolution of humanity. Ikeda Center programs include public forums and scholarly seminars that are organized collaboratively and offer a range of perspectives on key issues in global ethics. The Center was initially called the Boston Research Center for the 21st Century and became the Ikeda Center in 2009.

For more information, visit the Ikeda Center website: www.ikedacenter.org

Table of Contents

Kaneko Ikeda, Daisaku Ikeda, and Sarah Wider, Tokyo, 2006

Preface

"Poet, speak not with the intellect alone but with the 'flower of the mind'"[1]—such was the cry of the great nineteenth-century American poet and thinker Ralph Waldo Emerson, a flag bearer for the revival of humanity.

There has long been a call for the restoration in our world of the power of language, the power of literature, and the power of poetry. This is, at the same time, a warning of the underlying threat to civilization posed by the degeneration of heart-to-heart ties linking one individual to another. How, then, can we transform language from a meaningless, empty shell to the rich nourishment that sustains life, from being degraded as a dangerous tool for the exploitation of others into a powerful source for advancing into the future, filled with hope?

Sarah Ann Wider, former president of the Ralph Waldo Emerson Society, has been engaged in an earnest exploration of the essential question, "What enables us to lead fully and truly human lives?" She has been carrying on a dialogue, transcending the ages, with the thinkers who led the American Renaissance, deeply pondering their message.

I first met Dr. Wider in the summer of 2006. Her sincere character and profound integrity as a person shone brightly in each word she exchanged with me. My wife was moved to learn that the blue suit that Dr. Wider wore that day was a memento from her mother, Mary Wider. I was also touched when, later, Dr. Wider presented me with some of her mother's favorite books.

Dr. Wider told me that her mother read Emerson's essay "Self-Reliance" when she was in high school, which helped her decide not to be pressed into the conventional patterns imposed on women by society at that time but to follow her own chosen path through life. Motivated by her wish to be of use to a friend suffering from a serious illness, Mary Wider overcame numerous difficulties to enter one of the best nursing schools in the country. Through her devoted care, she helped her friend to live a longer life and went on to give the spiritual gift of hope and courage to many others who were ill.

In her later years, Dr. Wider also told me, her mother was gratified that her daughter chose Emerson as the focus of her academic career. I cannot help but feel that Dr. Wider and her mother are linked by the noble ideals voiced by Emerson—his unflagging belief in the infinite possibility of the individual and the supreme worth and dignity of our inner beings.

I have fond memories of the great spiritual sustenance and encouragement I received from the writings of Emerson and Walt Whitman in my youth. In those days, having accepted as my personal credo the impassioned wish of my mentor, second Soka Gakkai president Josei Toda, to rid the world of misery, I was engaged in an arduous daily struggle for peace based on the Buddhist teachings.

Serendipitously, the date July 3, when I first met Dr. Wider in 2006, is the same date that President Toda was released from prison in 1945, after being incarcerated for two years for his conscientious resistance to the dictates of the militaristic Japanese authorities. It is also the date that, twelve years later, in 1957, I was arrested on false charges in the midst of my efforts to expand our movement for the people's welfare.[2]

As long as people inherit and carry on noble ideals, these ideals will survive undimmed for eternity, eventually bringing glorious flowers into bloom and bearing fruit that stands as irrefutable proof in each person's life.

In July 2006, to commemorate Mary Wider, we planted a cherry tree—a favorite of my mentor—in the Makiguchi Memorial Garden adjacent to Soka University of Japan. Over the years, the tree has grown and bloomed beautifully, watching warmly over the university students as they have pursued their path of learning.

The British historian Arnold J. Toynbee, considering humanity's future, called for a new field of learning—a field that would employ the human intellect for good rather than evil, that would promote a way of life recognizing the equal worth and dignity of self and others. Based on his hopes for these "new humanities," Dr. Toynbee asked, "Are not these 'new humanities' likely to minister far more effectively than science and technology ever can to Man's present need to save himself from himself?"[3] I am convinced that this remains just as urgent an issue today as it was when these words were written more than four decades ago.

In our dialogue, focusing on the central theme of the revival of the poetic spirit and the restoration of the power of language, Dr. Wider and I explored many diverse subjects, including youth, women, friendship, art, literature, and the role of the university, tackling topics that Toynbee identified as the tug of war in education—the struggle between the often conflicting demands of national and economic interests on the one hand and individual and humanitarian interests on the other; between science and technology on the one hand and the humanities and arts on the other.

In our discussions, Dr. Wider noted that

> it is too easy to forget our responsibility to others when we're involved in an abstract quest for knowledge. . . . Then we start to neglect so much else in our lives. . . . When individualism is put in the service of materialism, we distort

the human being into a small-minded thinker who values acquisition over relation and self-selection over integral connection.

These ideas are profoundly consonant with the convictions I have held for many long years. I feel a special empathy with the ethos underlying Dr. Wider's observations and her profoundly compassionate spirit and deeply held belief as an educator in the need to dispel the dark clouds casting a pall over the lives of youth today. This is an unshakable pillar in Dr. Wider's view of education—a philosophy that stands as the epitome and culmination of the educational praxis in which she has so passionately engaged.

What can be done to prevent students from being swept away by the tide of the times and losing sight of their true selves? What kind of education can help them believe in their own potential and develop it to the fullest? All her ideas and actions derive from her wish for the happiness of each individual.

This desire is certainly the key to resolving the tug of war in education that Toynbee described. Wishing for the happiness of each individual and acting sincerely on this purpose—these qualities are desirable not only in education but in every area of our lives.

At the time of the March 11, 2011, earthquake and tsunami in Japan's Tohoku region,[4] Dr. Wider was quick to send a message. She asked what connects and strengthens us when we feel completely overwhelmed by the devastation around us, when it seems that everything is broken to pieces and torn apart. *Words of encouragement* was her answer. From far-away America, Dr. Wider felt the profound sadness of those in the affected areas and, reflecting on the grief she felt at her mother's death and her experience recovering from it, sent her sincere condolences and encouragement to all concerned.

When she visited Japan in October 2012, she traveled to Sendai, Ishinomaki, and Onagawa, sympathetically listening to the victims' stories and delivering lectures to ignite the torch of hope and courage in their hearts. She said that to communicate meaningfully with those who have experienced unbearable grief in the depths of their beings, our words must contain a power that transcends mere words. She concluded:

> In the aftermath of the earthquake and tsunami, the poetic heart responds again and again, from those who had suffered so much and from those who were suffering in deep sympathy. If we allow that heart its full power, there is no wasteland that cannot be transformed.

This sincere, heartfelt encouragement brought tears of deep feeling and empathy, and bright smiles of hope to the faces of many people. In order for Tohoku to shine even more brightly as a symbol of revival in the new century, I hope, along with Dr. Wider, that it will powerfully radiate this beautiful poetic heart.

It is also my sincere wish that this book will contribute to the rising tide of humanistic education, encouraging the "young Emersons" of our time to polish their minds and character for the sake of others, society, and the world.

With undying friendship on this seventh anniversary
of the July 3 on which I first met Dr. Wider,
Daisaku Ikeda

Preface

Every dialogue is a journey. Conversing, we begin, a few words at a time. Where will this thought lead? How will that observation deepen? In thought, we do not—we cannot—stand still. When we are thinking freely and frankly, we move. Especially when we are thinking together. Then that miracle of miracles occurs. We change our minds. We learn to see differently. Actively sharing thought with another person, we reach a place we could not reach alone.

That the focus of these dialogues with Daisaku Ikeda would turn to education is no surprise. I like to say I have been in school all my life, always a student, although for the last half of my life, I count teaching as part of my student's journey.

For President Ikeda, education is everything. Enabling education for others has been his lifework. As president of the Soka Gakkai International, the world's largest Buddhist organization, he realized the longtime dreams of its earlier leaders, Tsunesaburo Makiguchi and Josei Toda. Both wanted to create educational opportunities for people of all ages—not only opportunities but environments for learning that affirm and develop every student's creative potential.

At the core of realizing these dreams was not a "me-centered" individual but a long-visioned person building a peace-centered world of truly large understanding. The Soka schools around the world attest to President Ikeda's determination to see Makiguchi's and Toda's dreams become a lived reality for many students.

I had the great good fortune to meet President Ikeda and his wife, Kaneko, on a steamy July day in 2006 in Hachioji, Tokyo, at Soka University of Japan. We spoke briefly about our shared commitment to building cultures of peace in every moment. For me, this most often means in the classroom with my students. For the Ikedas, it includes their almost daily interactions—now, often through poems—with the students attending the Soka schools around the world.

Part of my trip in 2006 took me to those schools, meeting with their students, an opportunity I have been fortunate to repeat many times. I have heard junior high and high school students at the Tokyo Soka schools talk about the importance of cultivating imagination as a path to empathy; I have discussed Emersonian "conversations with nature" with students at both Soka University of America and Soka University of Japan. I have listened and learned from Soka Women's College students as they studied the poetry of Daisaku Ikeda, and I have parsed the difficult, circuitous language of Emerson's *Nature* with graduate students at SUJ.

Conversations with students at these Soka schools have been some of the most thought provoking of my life. This sounds like an exaggeration. It is not. These students have embarked on the mind-expanding life journey of dialogue.

When I was asked to join in a formal dialogue with President Ikeda, it was clear that we both felt the immediacy of our initial audience. Published first in *Pumpkin*, a Japanese magazine designed for women readers and the eclectic demands of women's daily lives, our words quickly opened into the larger educative demands that face us on a daily basis. How do we attend to, learn from, and in turn create something humane amid the multiple demands that fragment our days and may leave us feeling displaced and depleted?

Pursuing questions that address the human capacity for wonder, we let our minds wander among all places and times, inviting our readers to undertake their own journeys as well. What might the women of the American Transcendentalist movement teach us about how we attend to the mind's workings? How do Georgia O'Keeffe's life and work continue to challenge our ways of seeing? What are our responsibilities to where we are? What are the powers of poetry, and why have we neglected them?

Thought opens to thought. Every observation is just waiting to be shared and explored. Throughout the process, what grew in clarity was the collaborative nature of thought.

The dialogue process itself exemplified collaboration. First, the many occasions for dialogue at the Ikeda Center for Peace, Learning, and Dialogue or with the students at the Soka schools or with members of the women's and young women's divisions of the SGI created a rhythm of dialogue that opened happily and readily into this dialogue in particular. From the beginning, our thoughts were already used to traveling, to being in motion, given the freedom to ride on any train of thought that stopped at our dialogic station. In an interconnected world, there are no tangents.

Second, collaboration was built into the very way the dialogue proceeded. Much occurred via email exchange—each of us writing thoughts to which the other would in turn respond. We had time. We could always stop and think.

In addition, much of my thinking occurred in conversation with Masao Yokota, former president of the Ikeda Center. At a time when health concerns limited my writing and computer use, our conversations gave me the opportunity to expand and explore ideas, sharing in the fruitful give and take of thought. Grateful thanks also go to those who patiently transcribed the recorded conversations, especially to Clarissa Douglass, whose insight deepened and enriched the thoughts that would finally be written on the page. Such thought sharing would have been impossible without the translators who rendered English into Japanese, and Japanese into English. The gift of having one's thought rendered for others is incomparably precious, and in addition to the translators, my deep appreciation rests with everyone at the Ikeda Center. They provide a rare and precious home for dialogue.

Reflecting upon the time during which President Ikeda and I shared this dialogue journey, a landscape emerges. Here is a topography of education in all its multifaceted features. How have the current consumer-based models of education drained the human capacity for curiosity and creativity? How can these capacities be rejuvenated and encouraged? What is the role of compassion in education? And imagination? And empathy? How do thinkers, poets, artists from earlier ages—whether Nichiren, Emerson, Margaret Fuller, Rabindranath Tagore—most thought-provokingly enter the work we do in our daily lives? How do we continue to expand our understanding of education so that its dimensions remain inclusive and responsible? In a world of judgment and standards, how do we create and sustain a challenging and mind-expanding method based on respect, encouragement, and appreciation?

As I look out the tall library windows onto the windy summerscape of the college campus where I teach, I could translate these questions into the features I see around me, whether the blue heron just landing on the pond, or the clouds promising rain that would be more fully appreciated elsewhere, or the planted fields on the hillsides struggling for sunshine and warmth to allow the crops a chance to flourish.

Our campus is quiet in summer, and yet the work continues. Education never ends. Nor do the friendships begun and sustained through dialogue. Honoring education that nurtures and friendships that sustain, I celebrate Daisaku Ikeda and his buoyant and joyful commitment to learning, always learning. I invite you to join the journey and share your thoughts.

Dr. Sarah Wider

CONVERSATION ONE

New Adventures

IKEDA: The future is now; step forward, head held high with self-confidence, courage burning in your breast—and the moment you do, the breeze heralding a hope-filled future begins to blow.

I am reminded of the encouraging words of the philosophers of the American Renaissance. Ralph Waldo Emerson, whom I read in my youth, once wrote: "Build...your own world. As fast as you conform your life to the pure idea in your mind, that will unfold its great proportions."[1]

It was a dark time: Our former value system collapsed following Japan's defeat in World War II, and we did not know what to believe in. My family lost everything in the war. Our home burned in an air raid, and my oldest brother was killed in battle. I was physically weak, suffering from tuberculosis. In the struggle that was our daily life, I found tremendous encouragement in Emerson's urging to hold on to what I believed and strive for a better future.

Dr. Wider, you are not only a poet and educator, you are also an expert in Emerson studies. I am therefore delighted to begin this dialogue with you. Together I hope we can send a strong message of hope and courage to young people seeking to live a correct life in this present era of major transition. I'd like to explore Emerson's life and thought, then broaden our discussion to include modern literature and the essence of humanistic education. In addition, I hope you will share with us your thoughts on the new century of women from the feminine and maternal viewpoints.

WIDER: Thank you for your encouragement. I am extremely grateful for the opportunity to engage in this dialogue with you on issues that mean so much for our future. In a world in which inhumanity has gained the upper hand, we urgently need to encourage education consistent with human values. Now is a time to act with compassion, empathy, and clear-sightedness.

We so often look without seeing and hear without listening. These are days that demand great courage from each of us, and your opening words are both inspiring and inspiriting, inviting us to respond in hope, not fear, and to do what we can rather than be consumed by what we cannot.

IKEDA: As you so perceptively indicate, education consistent with human values will become increasingly indispensable. The depth of the education we can provide will be reflected in the depth of our society and our culture. Education is the fertile ground that enables humanity to blossom in all its fullness. From this perspective, I have made education my top priority, which has included founding the Soka Junior and Senior High Schools, Soka University, Soka Women's College, and Soka University of America.[2]

WIDER: During my visit to Soka University of Japan in July 2006, everyone greeted me with such kindness and enthusiasm that I immediately felt at home. Although it was our first meeting, I felt as comfortable with you and your wife as if we had known one another for years and had all the time in the world.

I had a feeling that my parents' spirits, too, were present. It was a wonderful moment that I cherish. Mom and Dad would have felt akin to the ideas we were discussing about the education of young people. Both of them believed strongly in wholeheartedly encouraging every young person to develop and always keep developing their potential.

IKEDA: I heard that the suit you wore at the time was a memento of your mother. My wife was moved to learn this.

By the spring of 2009, the cherry tree we planted in honor of your mother at the Makiguchi Memorial Garden next to Soka University had grown big enough to put forth fragrant blossoms. When I suggested the tree planting, you said your mother would be pleased because she loved trees and growing things. You added that you lacked words to say how happy the occasion made you, and that you felt like setting it to music. I still vividly remember everything you said.

On another occasion, you were kind enough to give me precious books your mother left to you. I have presented them to women of the SGI, who regard them as a treasure. These books reflect the profound love and respect you felt for your mother.

It is said that great people often have great mothers. What was your mother like?

WIDER: My mother, Mary, was enthusiastic. She embodied the Emerson quote, "Nothing great was ever achieved without enthusiasm."[3] She loved people and was deeply engaged and excited by what they were doing and happy for them in their endeavors. She radiated a sense of joy and a feeling that "I can do this!" I remember how she volunteered in the library at my school when I was a child and helped many students recognize their love of reading or research.

She was mentally robust and straightforward, and liked things to be direct and honest. She was also affectionate. I always felt comfortable hugging her. Especially when I was a child, when feelings are as tender as new leaves, it was easy to share feelings with her. Highly inquisitive, she just loved thinking about things.

IKEDA: I can see that she was a caring woman of great goodness who brought much love and joy to others. She was like the sun to you.

The lovely relation between you two reminds me of one of my poems, "A Symphony of Great and Noble Mothers":

> *Mothers are the sun,*
> *brightest of all.*
> *Mothers are the earth,*
> *infinitely bountiful.*
> *Mothers are the symbols of happiness,*
> *ever optimistic,*
> *walking tall with their heads held high. . . .*
>
> *Don't make mothers suffer!*
> *Protect mothers!*
> *Praise mothers!*
> *Don't belittle mothers!*
> *Give mothers*
> *all your support and love.*
> *That is the way of humanity.*[4]

WIDER: Your wonderful solar image pleases me because, in Western thought, women are often identified with the moon. The moon is beautiful, and I love it, but it is too often seen as dependent. I am glad to have women and mothers represented as the sun.

The sun is the source of all life on the planet. Women are positive, creative forces in their own right. For the child, the mother is light and warmth. She casts light for young persons as they grow into their own lives. She sends light so that the child can see how to go forward.

Another wonderful thing about the solar image is its outward-moving radiance. In this way, too, it conveys the image of an active and positive force.

IN LARGER TERMS

IKEDA: What you say is beautifully replete with the heartfelt respect you have for mothers. Your words will greatly encourage women throughout the world who work hard to bring up their children, who dedicate themselves to serving their families, communities, and society as a whole.

Speaking of the sun, I understand that the town where you were born and raised is a wonderfully sunny place.

WIDER: Yes, I was born in Albuquerque, New Mexico, which is now a big city but was still relatively small then. Across the street from our house was undeveloped land where roadrunners raced, then paused, only to dart away again, imparting their own rhythm to the land. I grew up with deep blue sky, vibrant sunshine, and lots of outdoor time. I loved being outside in New Mexico, where most of the year the weather is congenial.

I think of our house as filled with light—as, of course, in New Mexico it literally was. My father, Henry, was a very positive man who often said: "Had a good day yesterday. Gonna have a good day today. And gonna have a good day tomorrow." Every morning, he arose filled with tremendous energy. My mother was the same.

Every day was a new adventure. I loved the feeling of looking forward to whatever the day would bring. Mother was wonderful on special occasions like birthdays or holidays, so there was always something to look forward to. The house felt like a place where love lived.

IKEDA: You vividly depict a warm, cheerful home, illuminated with love. As Buddhism teaches, "One day of life is more valuable than all the treasures of the major world system."[5] Your parents were experts at life, living each day to the fullest, themselves filled with vitality and good cheer. And you say that every morning they arose filled with tremendous energy. Although at first this may not seem extraordinary, this is an important key to a victorious life.

My family cultured and produced nori (edible seaweed), and we had to be up early every morning. Although he was so stubborn that neighbors called him Mr. Hardhead, I remember my father as a good man who took good care of the people around him. Starting when I was in second grade, rheumatism confined him to bed for two years. This meant that our family business had to be cut back, reducing our income and putting the extraordinary burden of raising a large family on my mother.

She kept her spirits up and jokingly used to say, "We may be poor, but we're grand champions at being poor." I can still see her slight figure constantly, zealously working from the dark of dawn till late at night, never complaining and never resting, even when she caught cold. The sight of her silent labors taught me the value of work.

WIDER: As our American saying goes, she made lemons into lemonade. She certainly embodied the image of the sun we've been discussing. She brought warmth into your home and radiated light with her smile.

I learned attitudes toward work from my mother, too. She used to tell me that whatever a person does, it should be done enthusiastically, have a positive effect, and serve the interests of other people. Work should not be solely for oneself. We always need to be thinking in larger terms and beyond ourselves. This has been a tremendously important concept for me as a teacher and also as a parent.

IKEDA: Yes, it embodies a fine philosophy of life, a wisdom that is supremely essential in the world today. It provides a lofty guideline for living in a way consonant with the best of our humanity.

This is similar to the idea underlying Soka education.[6] I have regularly offered similar guidelines for our educational institutions, including Soka University and the Soka Junior and Senior High Schools in Japan and Soka University of America.

For instance, on the occasion of the opening of the Tokyo Soka Junior and Senior High Schools, I presented the students with the motto "Wisdom, Honor, and Passion," and established five guidelines, including "Become people who seek the truth, create value, and possess wisdom and enthusiasm."[7]

For the Kansai Soka Junior and Senior High Schools, which began as girls' schools, I offered the motto "Common Sense, Good Health, and Hope" and urged students to never build their own happiness on the misfortune of others.

At Soka University of Japan in 1971, I had two thought-provoking passages engraved on the pedestals of a pair of bronze groups, one depicting an angel and a printer, the other an angel and a blacksmith: "For what purpose should one cultivate wisdom? May you always ask yourself this question" and "Only labor and devotion to one's mission give life its worth."

Why should a person study? Not for himself or herself alone but to become the kind of person who can fulfill the noble mission of contributing to peace and the happiness of humanity. In this, I think your mother would agree with me.

BECOME STRONG!

WIDER: At Soka University in 2006, I had a chance to talk with students of Soka Women's College. A short experience, it nonetheless remains one of the most important elements in my life. It delighted me to spend time speaking with a group of young women who were clearly so glad—even excited—to be there and eager, keen, and participatory in their listening. I was impressed by their understanding that listening makes the listener part of what is happening. Without this, nothing being said matters. The students at Soka Women's College listened well and asked probing, thought-provoking questions.

On the first anniversary of our meeting, they sent me a beautiful album of the previous year. Others have sent me thoughtful cards and New Year's remembrances. In 2009, the students sent me a wonderful letter with vibrant photographs from their annual sports festival, which I carried with me when I visited Japan for the Toda Peace Institute conference,[8] in order to convey my joyous and heartfelt gratitude for the students' thoughtfulness. They also included a CD with two rousing renditions of their school song— the original in Japanese and the newly translated English version. I was so glad to hear their strong, cheerful voices. I greatly appreciate their ongoing thoughtfulness as well as their determination to become international women.

In December 2006, when I was invited to attend graduation ceremonies at the Calabasas campus of Soka University of America, I was delighted to have a chance to meet some of these wonderful young women again. When they told me that Japanese language is easy to learn, while English is difficult, I jokingly suggested they should teach me Japanese. There was no time, however, since they were returning to Japan the next day.

IKEDA: Thank you for sharing the experience. I am glad to learn of it. Students have told me how happy and moved they were to receive your warm encouragement.

In your lecture at Soka Women's College, "Walking the Road of Perfect Peace: Women's Work for the Twenty-first Century," you referred to Emerson's famous essay on heroism:

"Never strike sail to a fear,"[9] Emerson said. Even though the wind is blowing hard, and fear is in your heart, don't trim your sails because of that fear. . . . fear does not come naturally to women. Women are strong in mind and body and spirit and also know that we just don't have time to spend on fear. We are too busy giving comfort, listening . . .

If we start paying attention to the many strong women we know, you won't see any striking sails to fear. Many are sailing the seas, their voices speaking for peace and justice. . . .

I believe that all our work in this world is the work of making peace—wherever we are, in whatever ways we can. Each of us carries within us something unique we alone can contribute.

Your powerful message and valuable interaction with the students will remain golden inspirations all their lives.

WIDER: I found being with them most inspiring. These young women are learning a vital solidarity, grounded in commitment to social justice. Women supporting one another in such work are tremendously empowering, especially in a world that often limits and devalues women's intellect and insight. From what I can see, while Soka Women's College students work tremendously hard, instead of wishing for a lightening of their load, they are eager for more. Their motivation comes not from worry or concern but from the conviction, "We have important work to accomplish in and for this world."

I often see American students so afraid they will not find jobs or places after graduation. It seems hard for them to believe that they have a larger, world-changing lifework ahead of them. The Soka students I meet, on the other hand, never wonder whether there will be places for them. Their attitude is, "We will go forward; we know we have something to offer in creating a world of peace with social justice."

IKEDA: Thank you for your warm words. I am sure they will delight the students with whom you interacted, that recalling this experience will bring them renewed inspiration and vitality.

In October 2002, I delivered a lecture at Soka Women's College at the students' request. I offered these words of encouragement:

> Forge a solid self, and develop within you the power to attract happiness to your life. Then you will be happy and fulfilled, and you will lead your family, relatives and friends to happiness, too. We only live this precious life once. Please make continual efforts, steadily overcoming life's challenges one step at a time, until you ultimately achieve a life in which all of your wishes are realized.[10]

You, Dr. Wider, clearly possess the "power to attract happiness" to which I referred.

WIDER: I see two key, interrelated elements in what you say: A strong, solid self based on non-attachment leads to the power that attracts happiness. On the other hand, self-absorption blocks our happiness. Your words are profoundly significant and indicate a deep and expansive philosophy of life.

I have been encouraged by your words and thoughtfulness, like when you sent me your book of original poems and photographs *The Poet's Star*. The book arrived shortly before my mother died and kept me company through the winter of my grief.

That was when I had to rethink the nature of happiness. It is not some passive condition that arrives without your involvement but something you create. It emerges from the active struggle for peace with justice that is the real meaning of being a responsible, loving person in this world.

Poetry speaks directly to whoever is reading it. When I read your book, I felt a wonderful companionship. Its strong voice made me conscious of a real, immediate presence right there with me in the room, which was especially comforting just after I had lost someone who had been a precious presence throughout my life.

The words themselves were encouraging, especially the passage: "Become strong! Become strong! Become strong without fail! We need strength to be happy, to be victorious."[11] I read this passage many times. The words in no way minimized my difficulties, rather they showed me that strength resides within every struggle, waiting to be born.

IKEDA: I am honored to receive such kind words from a great poet like you.

As the flag bearers of the American Renaissance—including Emerson, Thoreau, and Whitman—showed us in their pioneering writings, language that is heartfelt and impassioned can transcend space and time, imparting the strength and hope to live. Moreover, it is a sharp sword of justice, keen enough to vanquish social evils.

As Walt Whitman wrote in *Leaves of Grass*:

> *"Camerado! This is no book,*
> *Who touches this, touches a man. . . ."*[12]

True poets, through the power of their personality and language, can dispel the darkness of our era and illumine humanity's path forward.

I believe that what our world needs most is the powerful, heartfelt cry of the human spirit, an awakening call for our time. This is the upwelling of true humanism and the restoration of the power of language to effect good.

I hope that our dialogue will shed light on both the thought and poetic spirit of the American Renaissance philosophers and on the beautiful spirit of women. I also feel that young people are participating in our dialogue, Dr. Wider, as we discuss the path we ought to pursue in the years to come.

CONVERSATION TWO

University of All Knowledges

IKEDA: A beautiful natural setting is a source of great happiness. The diverse events of the four seasons of life are colored by our natural environments, forming lasting memories deeply impressed on our minds.

You teach English literature and women's studies at Colgate University, the famous liberal arts institution. I feel a profound, marvelous connection with your school because an old friend is a member of the Colgate faculty. Colgate is located in the beautiful, historically significant village of Hamilton, in Madison County, New York, three or four hours' drive northwest of New York City. The town is named for Alexander Hamilton, one of the Founding Fathers of the United States.

What are your impressions of Hamilton?

WIDER: Wherever I am, I try to learn what the land itself has to tell us. Hamilton, for example, sits in a kind of valley common in upstate New York. Created by glaciers, such valleys remind us how magnificent masses of ice once moved across this land. Over the long course of time, the land that separates valley from valley has gentled into present-day, tree-covered hills.

Snow lies deep in winter, and summer offers more shades of green than I ever imagined. With our ample rains and snows, we are moisture-rich. Trees grow tall. From my study window, I can see a sugar maple—the same kind that is the source of our delicious maple syrup—rising to a towering height. My child, Taiward, calls it the "grandfather tree."

IKEDA: You paint a charming picture. The foliage of the sugar maples of the north country turns brilliant scarlet in the autumn. Just as surviving the hardships of winter makes spring lovelier, surviving the trials of life strengthens people and helps them develop a solid core.

I understand that Hamilton developed after the Colonies won independence from England.

WIDER: Our history goes back to the indigenous Haudenosaunee ("People of the Longhouse," known in French as the Iroquois)[1] through the post-Revolutionary period, the founding of the college, and the development of the Erie Canal. Unfortunately, as has been the case with many places in the United States, local history has been buried and sometimes even disdained, as if the past must be effaced for the future to arrive.

To know the place where you are requires a quality of thought, care, and interest not always encouraged within us. Too often, we take where we are for granted, rather than finding out about its natural and human history. What is the long continuum of the place in which we have this precious opportunity to participate? How will we use this opportunity?

As a college professor, I think about students who will live only a short while in a given place. To live well in a locality, we must be fully present and live deliberately and compassionately in it.

This is why I take such time and care with your question. If we take time, there is always room enough—room for the stories that have come before, room for those now unfolding, room for the stories yet to come.

IKEDA: Buddhism teaches:

> If you want to understand the causes that existed in the past, look at the results as they are manifested in the present. And if you want to understand what results will be manifested in the future, look at the causes that exist in the present.[2]

Past, present, and future are not three different things. We should use the past as a model for examining the present and illuminating the future.

I believe our current dialogue will be enriched by bearing in mind the trials and hardships experienced by our forebears. When Europeans arrived in North America, the Haudenosaunee lived mostly on the south shore of Lake Ontario and in upstate New York. Their advanced democratic principles are still worthy of our respect and admiration today. A core value of the Haudenosaunee has been, in every deliberation, to take into account the impact on future generations.

We should, with humility and sincerity, heed such lessons from traditional wisdom. In the areas of conservation and environmental issues, people today have much to learn from the knowledge and traditions of indigenous peoples. As you imply, this applies to communities all over the world.

WIDER: People grow within a place, and Hamilton presents a particular challenge. It is a population always in flux. Colgate students, most of whom live on campus rather than in the village, spend four short yet significant years in Hamilton. Almost without exception, Colgate faculty members have no ties to Hamilton before they arrive, and we increasingly face certain artificial demands in academic life that make it difficult to be literally where we are—in Hamilton, a place with a long natural and social history, among people whose tremendous knowledge can all too readily be overlooked and underappreciated by those who have recently arrived.

I often ask students, early in their college years, how each will connect with and appreciate a community in which they will live for only a short albeit meaningful duration. It is a difficult challenge, especially as colleges are now structured. There is still too much of the "ivory tower," where education is not integrally connected with the everyday realities of the place where the college is located. In the absence of these connections, students get busy with only their own lives in what they call the "Colgate Bubble," where parties and social posturing dominate.

As you can tell by the length of my response to your question, the interest I take in Hamilton expresses my distinct concern for this village in its many dimensions.

EVERY HOUR AND SEASON

IKEDA: Yes, I can see that. Students who have come to know and love Hamilton will no doubt regard this place where they studied in their youth as a precious second hometown. The Soka University students appreciate Tokyo's Hachioji, the town that is its home, and treasure the connections they make with local people there.

A university should contribute to the growth of the local culture. How to promote communication and exchange with neighbors and make a positive contribution to the community are regarded as important questions for Japanese universities, too.

In 2008, the Soka University Engineering Department developed a new variety of mulberry tree that has important uses in manufacturing health food. Hachioji is famous for its mulberry trees, and this new variety promises to help the growth and development of local industries, I am happy to say.

The peace scholar Elise Boulding told me that she taught her students to enthusiastically associate with local people and learn from them.[3] This is without a doubt an important way for students to discover new worlds.

Its lyrical, natural setting is one of Hamilton's most outstanding features. What is your favorite season there?

WIDER: Emerson said, "Every hour and season yields its tribute of delight."[4] I have experienced the full meaning of these words since I moved to Hamilton on an unexpectedly clear August day in 1986. No matter how cold the winter or how humid the summer, each season is distinctly beautiful. On days when the temperatures are far below freezing, the sun shines brightly in its winter radiance, and flakes of ice, the minute leaves of winter, grow from each tree branch.

Then, there are those hot summer days with their soft gray skies, when moisture lingers in the air but no rain falls from clouds to ground. As you can see, I have a difficult time picking a favorite.

We all love fall, with its rainbow of brilliant, many-colored leaves. Our trees grow resplendent in a range of golds, yellows, reds, oranges, and the still-persistent greens. Then, as the season wanes, the colors bronze in the descending light of autumn.

IKEDA: Your poetic description brings the panorama of the four seasons in Hamilton vividly to life. It is wonderful for a university to be located in such an enriching, natural setting.

I also believe an environment in which young people can become friends with nature, cultivating both the intellect and emotions, is important. This is why I chose not urban but suburban campus sites in beautiful natural settings for Soka University and the Soka Junior and Senior High Schools. We also hold summer school courses at both the Tokyo and Kansai Soka Junior and Senior High Schools, providing students the opportunity to experience nature—mountains, the sea, highlands, and wetlands—and study surrounded by the wondrous unfolding of nature.

WIDER: This is exceedingly important.

IKEDA: Our students enjoy it very much. In our program, elementary-, middle-, and high-school children learn about the wonder of life, the precious value of the natural world, and environmental issues, with rich natural settings around Japan as their classrooms: the Nasu Highlands in Tochigi, the Hiruzen Highlands in Okayama, the Tottori Sand Dunes, and so forth. These classes held in nature become the students' precious memories.

Emerson wrote: "We know more from nature than we can at will communicate. Its light flows into the mind evermore, and we forget its presence."[5] A familiarity with nature in youth and experiencing the amazing vitality of living things are important to character formation.

He wrote about his own childhood nature experiences: "I remember when I was a boy going upon the shore and being charmed with the colors and forms of the shells. I gathered up many and put them in my pocket."[6] Having grown up by the seashore, I have similar boyhood memories.

WIDER: Soka summer schools provide invaluable firsthand experience. There is no more powerful way to understand the importance and beauty of the natural world's diversity. During my visit to the Soka schools in Tokyo in June 2006, I greatly admired the marvelous learning environments, so wisely connected with nature. Such a way of life makes it far easier for students to learn deeply, with compassionate awareness of others.

On your campuses, I talked about the importance of imagination and learned a great deal from your students. They emphasized how imagination can put a positive spin on hardship. Using our imagination, we can see how to approach and resolve difficult situations creatively instead of fearfully. They also talked about the fundamental relation between imagination and empathy. Through imagination, they commented, we put ourselves in others' positions; we think with them and develop our ability to care for and about them. To this end, your students are enthusiastic about both study and extracurricular activities. Their enthusiasm and their insight into the imagination made me think I was observing modern-day Emersons.

IKEDA: Our students vividly remember your explanation that Emerson regarded friendship as something to be assiduously cultivated throughout life:

> Emerson said that friendship and friends exist in a place in which all barriers are transcended. We have many opportunities to learn, he said, but associating with a wide variety of people is the way to learn and foster true friendships. And if, as Emerson said, the individual mind is a "university of all knowledges," then friendship is one of the best ways to nurture and expand our knowledge and understanding.

Friendship as a way of encountering the "university of all knowledges" — that's a thought-provoking observation.[7]

Nichiren, the thirteenth-century Japanese Buddhist thinker and reformer whose teachings we in the Soka Gakkai embrace, uses the lovely expression "a friend of the orchid room," meaning that when two people engage in dialogue as good friends, they learn from each other and elevate themselves in the process just as anything in a room filled with fragrant orchids is perfumed by the flower's lovely scent. For Soka students, too, friendships made in youth often provide lifelong bonds, strength, and mutual support.

I understand that Emerson's study was full of seashells, fossils, and other objects from nature.

THE BEST EDUCATION

WIDER: Yes, it was filled with wonderful objects that children delight in, and he welcomed children into it. He set aside certain times of the day when children could be part of his "study life," and he was careful about how many children at a time. It generally was only one! But his rules were respectfully meant.

Emerson was an enthusiastic father who enjoyed children tremendously. According to one report, unusual for men of his class and time, if a baby was in the room, he wanted to hold this small person, so new to the world. His children remembered with warmth and affection the long walks they took with their father. On Sunday afternoons, Emerson would come into the front hall and either whistle or call out, "Four o'clock." Then all the kids in the house would gather. Sometimes neighbors' children, too, would tag along on four-to-eight mile strolls.

On these occasions, he loved pointing out seasonal phenomena or rare plants that might only recently have been identified, perhaps by their friend Henry David Thoreau. Emerson enjoyed those outdoor excursions just as much as the children. He believed strongly in the importance of children and in encouraging them to develop their powers of perception. He not only wrote about it, he lived it.

IKEDA: These walks were wonderful opportunities to study nature, to share thoughts and feelings, and to promote mental and physical health.

Josei Toda, my mentor and the Soka Gakkai's second president, always insisted that children should have frequent contact with nature. "Running around barefoot is good for children," he said. "It makes them strong."

City children have few such opportunities. These days, we rarely see children running and playing with their friends in open fields until the sun goes down. We should allow them more opportunities for unrestricted contact with the natural world. Though today children can learn about even the rarest plants through books, pictures, and the Internet, nothing can beat the experience of strolling through nature with family and friends, talking and learning in the midst of nature, in direct contact with its brimming vitality.

WIDER: As Emerson wrote, "There is so much, too, which a book cannot teach, which an old friend can."[8] Do you have any memories connected with particular plants near your home?

IKEDA: Yes, I have a memory of a cherry tree in our garden. When our second child was born, I moved with my wife and children to a house in Ota Ward, Tokyo, close to my parents-in-law. We planted a cherry tree in our small garden. It grew quickly, and by the time my oldest son was in middle school, it was quite large. I fondly remember sitting on our veranda with our whole family, chatting as we watched the cherry-blossom petals drift down. I explained to the children that the cherry tree is not originally from Japan but came from foothills of the Himalayas and was introduced to Japan from Korea, by way of the South Korean island of Jeju.

For a fairly long period after I became Soka Gakkai president (on May 3, 1960), I was too busy to return home more than three or four days a month. Still, it was important that, as much as possible, I find time to spend with my children enjoying nature, and I did my best to make the most of those opportunities.

Later, we moved to the Shinanomachi district of Tokyo, where the Soka Gakkai headquarters is located, and there were two cherry trees in our little garden. One spring, as we sat watching their petals dance down, my oldest son started a poem with the words "Blossom blizzard." I continued with "On the father's shoulders"; my wife completed it with "On the mother's hair." This haiku we composed together as a family is one of my fondest memories.

In Japan, cherry blossoms are regarded as the harbinger of spring hope. It had been my dream since my boyhood, which I spent in the dark days of wartime, to plant lots of cherry trees, symbols of peace. When I was young, a big cherry tree in my parents' garden always bloomed in an abundance of fragrant flowers. Gazing at its beauty, I dreamed of planting tens of thousands of trees at every train station throughout Japan.

WIDER: Your recollection of the poem your family wrote inspires me. Poetry is surely one of the strongest forces for good, especially when created together.

Conditions are different for each family, and parents cannot always be with children as much as they and the children would like. While children may feel closer to parents who make the effort to be with them as much as possible, it is not simply a matter of time. All too often, even given ample time, parents fail to build emotional connections with their children.

IKEDA: As the Japanese saying has it, children grow up with an eye on their parents' backs. Though they may not seem to be, children are always watching their parents closely. When the example and actions of parents inspire pride—even if the parents have only limited time to share with their children—this can provide the best education. Such an education is one of the great gifts in life that parents can give to their children.

Buddhism compares life to an unsurpassed jewel equal in value to the whole universe. Children possess boundless value and potential. Their lives are precious stones that shine brighter the more they are polished. Adults must not cloud the luster of these precious stones. I am convinced that the sight of their parents working and giving their all to others and their communities illuminates children's minds and makes their lives radiant.

CONVERSATION THREE

The Encouraging Voice

IKEDA: I am pleased to say that our dialogue on humanistic education from the perspective of women and the poetic spirit has aroused great interest,[1] especially regarding your wonderful description of your relationship with your mother (see Conversation One).

In all times and places, mothers are our greatest instructors, teaching us life's fundamentals. For children, the home is the first classroom. As the great hero of nonviolence Mahatma Gandhi said, "Every home is a university and the parents are its teachers."[2]

In this conversation, I want to discuss topics like family ties, the wisdom needed in childrearing, the importance of encouragement, and the pleasure of reading.

WIDER: I am delighted to hear that many readers find our dialogue stimulating and am grateful to you for asking about my upbringing and home environment. True exchanges of opinion are impossible unless the parties involved know something about each other. And in turn, the participants in a dialogue like this must reach out to their readers, inviting them to join in the thought process and take part in and continue the discussion. Only then does dialogue have the power to cultivate peace and promote a philosophy of compassionate understanding throughout the world. I will be especially pleased if our dialogue can encourage young mothers in the daily hard task of nurturing their children and supporting them in the ways of peace.

IKEDA: In a memorable passage, Emerson wrote, "Respect the child. . . . Be the companion of his thought, the friend of his friendship."[3] Emerson stressed the importance of parents helping their children to develop their inherent potential and goodness to the fullest. Instead of adopting the role of authoritarian disciplinarians, he urged parents to become their children's best friends.

You devote yourself enthusiastically to activities for the sake of peace and education. I feel sure that you must have many memories of profound exchanges with your wise parents in the spirit of the friendship advocated by Emerson. You mentioned that your father was an optimistic, cheerful person (see Conversation One). How did you and he relate when you were a child?

WIDER: He worked from morning till night and came home tired at the end of each day. Still, he often found a way of incorporating my sister or myself into his time to relax, even if only a brief measure by the clock. As a child, I felt proud of my father for the work he was doing. I think it is extremely important for parents to understand this: We give our children a great gift when we show them how our work contributes to others.

Not all work, however, is helpful to others. What about people engaged in jobs they cannot value and in which they can take no pride? What about people engaged in work that is life-diminishing instead of life-expanding?

Too many examples come to mind; they cross all barriers of societal positions. For example, the sex trade remains a flourishing industry. Sickeningly, it is one of the places where women can reliably obtain employment. Their jobs are based on exploitation, but they are not alone. Consider those who risk their lives daily in the industries based on mineral extraction. They would change their work if they could, but they must earn some sort of wage to support their family.

Or perhaps they do highly valuable work that society ignores. As famous singer and activist Paul Robeson reminded the construction workers for the Sydney Opera House in Australia, *they* were the builders; it was not the architects or the financiers.[4]

IKEDA: Yes, the demands of modern society can be harsh. Many people experience deep frustration with their careers. Nevertheless, we mustn't allow our work or our situation to define our lives.

My mentor encouraged young people having trouble at work by referencing his own mentor, Tsunesaburo Makiguchi, the first Soka Gakkai president. Makiguchi taught that there are three kinds of value: beauty, benefit, and good. In the working world, the value of beauty means to find a job we like; the value of benefit means to get a job that earns a good salary, so we can support our daily lives; and the value of good means to find a job that helps others and contributes to society. Toda said, "Everyone's ideal is to get a job they like (beauty), that offers financial security (benefit) where they can contribute to society (good)."[5]

Few people, however, can immediately find ideal jobs that fulfill all these requirements. Toda explained further that, rather than being discouraged by this, the most important thing is first becoming indispensable wherever we are. This will open the path leading to a victorious future. Then, when we look back, we will see how all our efforts have become precious assets.[6]

Most of the leaders and thinkers around the world I have met with stressed that all struggles in youth become treasures in life. I especially remember the Soviet novelist Mikhail A. Sholokhov:

Unable to graduate from middle school because of the Russian Revolution, he studied on his own while laboring as a stonemason, a stevedore, and in other jobs. His harsh experiences provided nourishment for his development as the author of great books, including *And Quiet Flows the Don*.

I met him on my first visit to the Soviet Union, in September 1974. He was sixty-nine, and I was only forty-six, and he welcomed me warmly, telling me:

> People who are not committed to reaching any firm goals are essentially powerless. We are all the forgers of our own happiness. Realizing happiness comes down to how much we have forged ourselves spiritually. Those who have inner fortitude can move their lives in a positive direction even when confronted with the vagaries of fate.[7]

Your father was also a man of conviction who forged his own happiness.

THIS YOUNG SPIRIT

WIDER: As my father often said, "There are no problems, only opportunities." While there were many difficulties in his job, he was happy in his work in New Mexico because he often felt he was providing jobs for people who might otherwise be unemployed. He loved encouraging others, especially young people of high-school and college age. He saw so much potential in them. He felt that, if you give them timely encouragement, the sky is the limit for what young people can achieve. And he believed people have the capacity to remain young all their lives.

I have so many wonderful memories of my father's encouragement. Soon after I started playing the cello, I was chosen to perform a small solo in a school concert. My father had to travel frequently for his work and couldn't possibly get home for the event. Nonetheless, he sent me a telegram. To be a nine-year-old receiving a telegram! I was amazed and honored, and have kept it to this day.

IKEDA: It must be one of your most treasured possessions. As your moving story makes clear, your father obviously loved, cared, and thought deeply about you.

I often used to send telegrams to encourage my friends and fellow Soka Gakkai members. I took time to write to them as well. And, wherever I went in Japan or anywhere else in the world, I always sent my children postcards. Though the messages were simple, I was careful to address cards to each child. I had made a commitment to myself that, as a father, no matter how busy I became, I would always do everything possible to keep the promises I made to them. One of these promises was to dine out with the whole family as often as possible. Although sometimes I could take only limited time from my schedule, I faithfully joined my wife and our children around the restaurant table whenever I could. Even when my next appointment forced me to leave after a short while, my wife, to encourage our children, always expressed her pleasure at my having found time to keep my word and be with them.

On occasions like birthdays, my wife sometimes prepared the gifts, and I gave them out when I got home. I am grateful to her for the support she provided in arranging even brief occasions that would create lasting memories with my children.

WIDER: Mrs. Ikeda's distinct and thoughtful care speaks eloquently of her understanding about how to work creatively under demanding circumstances, and you were never too busy to show your children your love.

As your life clearly shows, keeping promises to children is fundamental. It develops trust, that vital component in human relationships. Children remember going out with the family, even on minor occasions.

Among my memories of childhood, special concerts stand out especially vividly. I am still thrilled to recall that my parents trusted me, as a five- or six-year-old, to sit still and listen to the music. On my seventh birthday, as a treat, they took me to a concert by the Philadelphia Orchestra, conducted by Eugene Ormandy. I distinctly remember the enormity of the sound, the decided-yet-flowing movements of the conductor, and the sight of a stage filled with musicians creating music.

Ikeda: Eugene Ormandy and the Philadelphia Orchestra rank among the greatest pairings of twentieth-century orchestral art. I heard that Ormandy started studying the violin at the age of two. I also heard that his father, a dentist, was so strict that little Eugene had to read his favorite books behind his father's back.[8]

Wider: I started piano lessons when I was not quite five. I never considered practicing a chore. My sister, Susan, played the violin, and as I grew better on the piano, I often accompanied her.

When I was a junior in high school, our orchestra was given the wonderful opportunity to go to Europe. Dad was one of our chaperones. At St. Mark's Basilica in Venice, two of my friends and I became so engrossed in close examinations of the mosaics that we completely lost track of time and caused our group to miss the water taxi back to the hotel. My friends' fathers were angry with them. But, after I explained and apologized for my carelessness, my father said simply, "I understand." He honored my youthful curiosity and interest, and did not want to cramp it. I was happy that he didn't humiliate me in front of my friends. Whenever he wanted to say anything critical of me, he always said it in private.

IKEDA: His subtlety in such personal relations suggests that he was a great humanistic educator. Delicacy and innovative thinking strengthen the emotional bonds and trust between parents and children. Exploring the world with your children with an inquisitive spirit is also one of the joys and missions of parenting.

My mentor used to say that, because they can be fearsome to children even when silent, fathers should never scold children over minor matters.

What you say of your father reminds me of an incident connected with the great French poet Victor Hugo. In 1869, during his exile on the Isle of Guernsey, he arranged a party for forty underprivileged neighborhood children.[9] Addressing the adults present, he said:

> The child must be our concern. Do you know why? Do you know his true name? His name is The Future. . . . Whatever we do for children, the future will return to us a hundredfold. This young spirit, the child, is the field of future harvest. His life contains the future of society. Let us sow in this young spirit the seeds of justice, the seeds of joy. In raising this child, we are raising the future.

Children are not their parents' property: They are the future of humanity, the hope of the world. I have always believed that we must raise our children with this in mind. The foundation of education should be trust in and love for children, combined with stimulation and inspiration—as embodied by your father, who so eagerly protected and developed your curiosity and watched affectionately over you.

WIDER: For home to live up to its most vibrant potential, it is important that parents and children develop thoughtful respect and trust. Together they build an environment where every person can freely express himself or herself. Part of that respect arises from the parents' sustained, good-hearted willingness to cultivate and share their children's interests.

BUILDING RELATIONSHIPS

IKEDA: Your mention of mutual respect between parents and children calls to mind the relationship between Emerson's mother and her children. Emerson's father, who was a pastor, died young. His mother, Ruth Haskins Emerson, faced great hardships in raising her family.

WIDER: Parents often face daunting circumstances. Emerson's mother, Ruth, lost her husband, William, when her children were still quite young—Ralph Waldo was only eight. She had four sons to educate and another son with significant learning disabilities. Her task would be hard enough today, but the societal constraints of her time imposed unfair burdens on her and on her search for work that would support her family and further her sons' education.

It is sad that these burdens continue to fall on many women to this day. The "second shift" remains the norm; women continue to do most of the housework, no matter what their commitments in the workplace. And domestic work, particularly if it is done by women not part of the home, rarely is valued at its true worth.

Parents still ask whether a daughter's education is useful. Just recently in one of my classes, students reported comments they had heard that it was not worth educating a woman if she were going to become a housewife. From girlhood through womanhood, we are still all too often asked to "think like a man" and criticized as weak or inferior if our ways of thinking differ from that supposed standard. Women continue to do most of what sociologists call the "affective labor"—the emotional care of others that is absolutely vital to our health and yet requires energy as well as creativity and insight.

Mrs. Emerson remained deeply committed to her sons' education, as her husband had been, and happily called upon her brilliant sister-in-law Mary Moody Emerson[10] to oversee the young boys' learning. At the same time, Mrs. Emerson did not neglect her own education. Though making ends meet was difficult, she nonetheless set aside time every day to read the books that mattered to her. Observing this must have been important to Ralph Waldo in establishing lifelong reading habits and in forming his attitude toward other people's reading.

IKEDA: In Japan today, our print culture is in decline. In an effort to reverse this trend, some young mothers have originated a movement to encourage reading aloud to small children. The movement is spreading in creative ways throughout the country.[11] What you say about Emerson's mother should encourage them.

Mothers deserve our deepest gratitude. They are wonderful beings who give children the hope and courage they need in life, no matter what adversity must be faced.

Mikhail Sholokhov's mother lost both parents when she was young, had no chance for an education, and was illiterate. When her son Mikhail went far away to study, however, she learned to read and write so she could correspond with him. Behind the great writer was a mother's great love.

I understand that, with her profound affection and deep faith, Emerson's mother also greatly influenced his religious views.

WIDER: Emerson's mother kept records of the books she read. It is interesting that she loved devotional reading from all denominations, always preferring those that emphasized practical expressions of faith. She believed that faith must arise from a person's own experience and careful reflection. Emerson's biographer Robert D. Richardson has commented on her role in helping Emerson form his understanding of religion as something arising from within, not dictated by an institution.[12]

IKEDA: In Emerson's famous "Divinity School Address," he sharply criticized formalistic beliefs and called for a return to the original spirit of faith. The example of his mother's religious beliefs and attitudes is clearly reflected in the undercurrent of Emerson's thought.

Despite great challenge, Ruth Emerson managed to send Emerson as well as two of his brothers to Harvard. It must have required incredible effort on her part.

Her view of life is revealed in the following: When Emerson's older brother William arrived at Harvard, he complained in a letter to his mother of the poor conditions in Harvard dormitories. Ruth wrote back, gently chiding and encouraging him, saying that he should not trouble himself over trivia and should keep his aspirations high:

> MY DEAR SON, —You did right to give me so early a proof of your affection as to write me the first week of your College life. Everything respecting you is doubtless interesting to me, but your domestic arrangements the least of anything. . . . You, I trust, will rise superior to these little things, for though small indeed, they consume much time that might be appropriated to better purpose and far nobler pursuits. What most excites my solicitude is your moral improvement and your progress in virtue.[13]

The character of an astute, broad-minded American woman is reflected in this letter, which must have awakened her son to the great wisdom and large heart of rising above little things.

WIDER: As would have been customary at the time, Emerson's mother kept her emotions to herself. But on one occasion, when Waldo and William were unduly late returning home, she expressed her distress, bursting out, "My sons, I have been in an agony for you." Emerson said he went to bed "in bliss" that night knowing how much his mother cared.[14]

By the way, Emerson preferred his middle name, Waldo, to his first name, Ralph, and began using Waldo during college. He never gave a direct explanation why, though others have speculated. There were other Ralphs in the family, and the duplication of name could be confusing. There was also a sect deemed heretical in the twelfth century by the Catholic Church for its challenge of institutional authority. Its members were called Waldensians after the group's founder, Peter Waldo.

Ruth Emerson's household was poor in material goods but rich in intellect and spirit. Today's emphasis on material wealth bodes ill. Certainly in the United States, success is too often defined as affluence, the extent of one's possessions, and a certain lifestyle characterized by a large home and dominated by individual-use technology. Such a system is good at consuming resources but does little toward building and sustaining relationships.

The creative work of nurturing relationships does not require inordinate financial resources. In fact, such so-called resources often get in the way of what Emerson called "true relations."[15] Such relations take creativity, time, and energy. Their true resource is wise and honest encouragement from parents, grandparents, siblings, and friends.

Building relationships is a powerful, creative art. If as much time had been given to the art of relationships as has been given to other dimensions of our society, we might be in a different place today.

IKEDA: Nichiren wrote, "More valuable than treasures in a storehouse are the treasures of the body, and the treasures of the heart are the most valuable of all."[16] In its headlong pursuit of the "treasures in a storehouse," in the flood of knowledge and information inundating us, materialistic modern society has lost sight of the "treasures of the heart."

Nichiren also teaches that "'joy' means that oneself and others together experience joy"[17] and "both oneself and others together will take joy in the possession of wisdom and compassion."[18] In other words, true happiness comes from contributing to the welfare of others and society—*in sharing joy.* I believe that this creative way of life is the key to the restoration of our humanity. You, too, have stressed the importance of encouragement in family, school, and society.

Indeed, a single word of encouragement from parents, siblings, teachers, seniors, or friends can dramatically alter a person's life. It can impart hope to live and strength to overcome hardships. Encouraging others can be described as enabling the inner strength, the inner power, of others to shine.

The Danish poet laureate Esther Gress, who was a friend of mine, sent me the following poem, of which I am fond:

One little word
can change
a world
for good.

One little word
can change
a man
for good.

Let's make the world
change us

all for
the good

Let us make the bells call

As you so beautiful are writing
Let us bring together
The toning chimes of peace
Rung from bell towers
of the world's poet.

Following the model of your revered mother and father, it is my wish to join with others in treasuring the encouraging voice, carrying it to society as a whole, and making it a great force for the creation of a better life.

WIDER: Taiward and I will treasure your thoughts about my parents, as we, too, seek to treasure the encouraging voice. And with my students, we will listen to Esther Gress's forthright reminder that our words matter, that we, too, can speak world-changing words and together ring the "chimes of peace."

CONVERSATION FOUR

All Things Connected

IKEDA: With the arrival of the first cold of winter, the moon shines with greater brilliance in the clear night sky. Nichiren compared the moon's radiance to the enlightening effect that true philosophy has on the human mind in troubled times: "The moon shines more brightly around dawn than it does in the early evening, and is more luminous in autumn and winter than in spring and summer."[1]

In Japan, there is a long tradition of appreciating the moon's beauty while sitting outdoors with family members and conversing or composing poetry. There is also a traditional moon-viewing celebration in the autumn, when people view the harvest moon and make offerings of pampas grass and dumplings. In my busy schedule, I have found time for such celebrations with international students.

The moon's expression changes constantly throughout the four seasons. I imagine the moon must look beautiful in the clear skies over Hamilton.

WIDER: I appreciate your description of the autumnal moons and Buddhism's wise understanding of when its luminosity is greatest.

Because Hamilton is often rich in clouds, full moons are special treasures. In particular, the autumnal moons, through their brilliant yellow-gold light, carry strength and courage for the winter. We should all take a lesson from traditional Japanese culture and cultivate such affection for the moon's light. I have seen in your photographs how vibrantly you see the moon's brightness.

IKEDA: Thank you for saying so. As a matter of fact, I started my nature photography with some pictures I took of the moon forty years ago. I was a little unwell at the time, and a friend, wishing to offer me a refreshing diversion, gave me a single-lens reflex camera. As an expression of my thanks, I sent him some photos I had taken. That's when I started keeping my camera handy at all times.

In June 1971, I visited Onuma Lakeside, in southern Hokkaido, to commemorate the completion of a Soka Gakkai training center. Having finished preparations for the following day's opening ceremonies, I was taking a drive around the area, when I suddenly noticed a glow rising into the night sky from behind some distant mountains. The people with me thought it might be the lights of a nearby town, but as we drove toward the light, we caught sight of a great round moon shining through breaks in the clouds. Its light made the ripples on the lake sparkle gold and silver.

I knew the moment was exactly right, had the driver stop the car, and clicked my camera shutter several times, capturing the panoramic beauty of the cosmos. This experience inspired me to begin recording nature in its various seasons in photographs.

WIDER: Your description brings that mystical moment to life. These references to the moon remind me of an incident in my mother's life. As a girl of four or five, spending time in the old family home in Maine, she saw moonlight as she lay in bed and asked her grandmother and aunt, "Can I get up to see the moon?"

She always loved watching the moon, and later, when she

related the incident to me, asked: "Do you realize how few full moons we will actually be able to see in our lives? We should make certain that we are always watching out for them. Never miss a full moon." I recall this vividly because it reveals how Mother valued paying attention, certainly to people but also to nature and everything around us.

IKEDA: This anecdote communicates your mother's deep sensitivity and a spirit as beautiful as moonlight. I'm certain you've inherited her poetic sensibilities and warm heart to a profound degree.

It is now more than thirty years since I composed the children's poem "The Moon's Wish," with this passage:

> *From fairyland, the moon . . .*
> *Are you studying hard?*
> *Are you good to your mothers?*
> *The smiling moon, who sees everything,*
> *sends you greetings.*

I think this overlaps with your mother's beautiful recollection.

Nature possesses a vitality and profundity that always enrich, beautify, and comfort the human heart. Emerson wrote, "The greatest delight which the fields and woods minister, is the suggestion of an occult relation between man and the vegetable. . . . They nod to me, and I to them."[2] When I converse with nature through my camera, I feel the same way. When I turn my lens toward a flower, I feel as if the flower were smiling back at me.

Just as each moment in our lives is unique, no two moments in nature are the same. Though flowers may seem to bloom in the same way year after year, in fact they are never the same as they were. What I see through my camera is an ever-changing, priceless world coming into being, then disappearing, moment after moment. I hope to capture this momentary beauty produced by nature and leave a lasting record. This, I believe, is what the art of photography can achieve—it's with this intent that I take my photographs.

WIDER: You crystallize this approach in all the wonderful photographs you take. Each is beautiful and speaks from a particular time and place to the viewer, wherever his or her thoughts and perceptions reside. I have come to know your photographs mostly through the books that so harmoniously combine the beauty of the visual image with the power of your words. These books are cherished gifts that have become wonderful companions.

You enable us to see that, throughout existence, all things are connected, often in immediate ways but just as often in subtle ways that we may fail to appreciate. Calling our attention to such interconnection, you remind us that we as human beings have much to learn from the world and much to give in return.

My mother was fond of saying, "Living is a wonderful experience." I associate the word *wonder* closely with her. When something caught her attention, she would inhale, then say, "The wonder of it all!" She taught by example to value and be grateful for the wonder in everything.

IKEDA: She offered you a wonderful insight into the true nature of life. When fully engaged with each event unfolding before you, you are always making new discoveries and can transform everything into a source of joy. The mirror of a beautiful heart reflects a world of beauty. A truly beautiful person can fully perceive and appreciate the world's beauty. This is the lesson your mother was teaching you.

Photography is a struggle to engage with the object being photographed as it changes moment by moment. In a sense, the same can be said of life: The important thing is to appreciate to the fullest the value of the events unfolding before you and the people you encounter.

Throughout his life, my mentor fully appreciated each person he encountered. He was deeply committed to bringing happiness to everyone he met, without exception. This was the way he lived from the time he was an elementary school teacher. Even after moving to Tokyo, he continued to correspond with the first students he had taught when starting out as an elementary-school teacher in Mayachi, Hokkaido. He invited some of them to Tokyo, where he helped them find work. Learning that one of his best students was unable to go on to higher education because of financial difficulties, he encouraged him by sending a dictionary.

The Soka Gakkai's foundation today is our leaders' continuance of Toda's approach—listening attentively to members' problems, warmly encouraging, supporting, and helping them. With such encouragement, these individuals have, through Buddhist faith and practice, rejuvenated their lives.

As heirs to my mentor's spirit, my wife and I pray and act daily for the good health, long life, and safety of the members. One of the most important teachings of the Lotus Sutra is to respect each individual as one would a Buddha.[3] Wherever I go, I use whatever free moments I can find to take photographs as gifts, hoping to bring happiness to the local members and residents.

WIDER: As a fellow educator, I find what you say about Josei Toda to be an inspiring reminder of how we should be with one another. In addition, what you say about your photography renews my awareness of the attentive care you devote to others.

THE MYSTERY OF LIFE

IKEDA: To return to the subject of valuing each individual, I believe that this approach applies to raising children. Children grow so rapidly that parents are certain to make fresh discoveries and observe new growth on a daily basis.

The Western-style Japanese artist Ryusei Kishida spent more

than ten years painting a series of portraits of his daughter, Reiko, that has become his most famous work. He began the series while recovering in the country from an illness. Even though he was in poor physical shape, the mystery of life, manifested in his daughter as she grew and changed day by day, seems to have stimulated his creative drive.

A parent doesn't have to be a painter, however, to experience wonder and inexpressible joy in observing how, unexpectedly and imperceptibly, children grow. Through this constant stream of new discoveries, childrearing becomes a means for the parents' own growth. In the midst of the pressing demands of daily life, and while keeping a watchful eye on their children and discovering new things about them, parents need to share their children's joys and worries, studies and progress. The important thing is for parents to learn from and grow together with their children.

What do you think is most important in raising children?

WIDER: In raising Taiward, I think I have devoted most of my attention to fostering hir creativity (you will see that I will be using the gender-neutral pronouns *hir* and *ze*). My joy as a mother has deepened as I have watched Taiward grow into hir own strong identity. The societally gendered norms never fit. In fact, they were downright suffocating.

Ze knows a world much larger than the either/or binaries so often imposed on us. As Taiward has come to understand who ze is and what is essential for hir true and creative self, ze has shown me yet again how crucial it is for all people to fundamentally be who they are.

When Taiward was younger, ze was always making something. It reminded me of my grandmother, who did the same. Now ze makes music playing cello in different ensembles, playing guitar, writing songs.

Most important is respect from parent to child. We all need to feel respected, especially by the people closest to us.

I knew I would be traveling to Japan in the summer of 2006. Taiward, who was going on eleven at the time, decided ze wanted to send a gift to you and your wife, something that ze had made. It was a small figure ze called the Peace Fairy. Ze made it from wood and flower petals, and was particular about the color because ze associates both feelings and ideas with color. Ze chose blue, the color of peace. Ze knew that I was going to be talking with people who have devoted their lives to peace. Presenting the figure Taiward had crafted made me feel as if ze was actually with me, and of course everybody was always asking about hir. It was wonderful to feel like I was sharing this.

IKEDA: Yes, I remember it well. I felt the beautiful blue doll embodied your child's gentleness and purity of heart. My wife, too, was delighted by hir unexpected, extremely sincere present.

WIDER: I am happy that it pleased you both. I look forward to the day when Taiward and I can travel together to Japan.

I think about how much Taiward has grown in the years since I delivered hir vibrant affirmation of peace. As you say, change happens daily, and we must keep our eyes, minds, and hearts open. Even at the stage sometimes called the "terrible twos," children aren't "terrible"—only inquisitive, energetic, and eager to find out what they can do. It was sometimes trying and certainly tiring for me, but even then, Taiward's necessary and natural growth compelled my respect. I've always wanted to communicate to hir a sense of how much I respect hir, and that I am eager to listen to hir thoughts, ideas, and feelings.

IKEDA: This is most important. Even when parents' heavy workloads and domestic duties make it hard, and in spite of all the patience and thoughtful care children require, the joys of raising children are immense. Parents often have such high, even excessive expectations and hopes for their children, for their futures or careers, that the parents can be highly emotional when they compare them to other children. But the most important thing, as you show, is to have deep, strong communication with your children to help them establish a firm foundation for their character.

A Buddhist parable (from the Sutra of One Hundred Parables) illustrates the importance of such foundation work: Once a rich man visited the home of another wealthy man. He was so impressed by its magnificence that he decided to build one even larger and more magnificent. He called builders and asked them to erect a grand, three-story residence, grander than the one he so admired. After some time, he visited the construction site, where he found the workers laying the foundation. Displeased, he cried out: "All I want is the third story. I don't care what's under it!" The disgusted builder carefully explained to him that you can't build a second story without building the first, and you can't build a third story without building the second. He and his workers, he said, were doing the preparation that was needed for the magnificent third story.

In all things, it's the foundation that is important. Education, too, begins with learning the foundations upon which we must build our lives.

WIDER: This story illustrates an important point. Certainly, day-to-day childrearing is hard, but it also brings irreplaceable gladness. For me, the greatest happiness comes when I hear Taiward talk about something that matters to hir and excites hir. At such times, I see hir growing stronger, settling into hir own potential, at ease in hir own world. It is wonderful for me as a parent to hear hir say things like "I'm happy" or "I like my life." I value these moments tremendously.

When people feel contented, they find courage for the good work they are uniquely able to do. They appreciate, you might say, their own *content*—the varied thoughts, imaginings, and experiences they contain. In this appreciation can be found contentment and a firm grounding for the growth of their potential.

I also value and consider powerful the moments when something is bothering Taiward, and we talk about it. I am grateful to have earned hir trust and delighted to see that ze is becoming an adept problem-solver hirself.

EMPATHY GROWS

IKEDA: For children, naturally impressionable and emotional, a trusted, dependable mother who carefully looks after them is a life foundation providing a powerful sense of security and stability. Your description of your experiences with your child will, I'm sure, be useful for many mothers.

I have spoken with mothers about the importance of making the home a haven of security and a beacon of happiness for children. The home needs to be a safe harbor to which our children can return throughout their childhood, school years, and on into the process of achieving adulthood—both when they have positive, happy experiences and when they face challenges and difficulties. A warm, supportive home environment that provides opportunities to share and communicate freely gives children self-confidence and enables them to manifest their strengths fully.

In September 1992, in our discussion on primary education, Necdet Serin, former rector of Turkey's Ankara University, told me:

> [Elementary education's key role is] to give children self-confidence in order to develop their creativity. Helping children to develop confidence in themselves, to trust themselves, enables them to grow in their capabilities. . . . Once their creative powers have been unlocked, children will study on their own and teachers won't have to guide

them through every step of the learning process any longer.[4]

WIDER: Creativity is the heart of learning. I love discussing things with Taiward, and I try my best to keep the discussion free of condescension. I also think children need to understand that their mothers are real human beings with feelings. It is vital to create relations in which children can understand how their parents feel.

Empathy grows with practice. Children are ingenious when it comes to comforting parents. They find it easy. I think there is no better feeling for a child than, "Oh, I've just cheered Mommy up!" They definitely know how.

IKEDA: Another Buddhist tale is about a king named Rinda, who is said to have acquired and maintained his dignity and strength by listening to the neighing of white horses, which neighed only when they saw white swans. When this story is applied to our discussion, the swans can be compared to children, the white horses to parents, and the king to the community. The smiling faces of children make parents happy and result in happy families that extend their influence to the community and then brighten society as a whole. In this sense, children are the treasures and the hope of society.

Ever since I founded the Soka elementary schools in Tokyo and Osaka, I have stressed the importance of recognizing that children, despite their relative lack of maturity, are full-fledged individuals. I have urged teachers to bear this constantly in mind in their interactions with them.

More than thirty years ago, at the opening of the Sapporo Soka Kindergarten in Hokkaido, I greeted students at the front entrance. I welcomed them each to the school, thanked them for coming, and asked them to get along with their fellow students, shaking the hand of each student. I visited their classrooms, where I sat in the same small chairs the children used, and once I rode the school bus with them and saw all of them safely home. I have heard that they all have fond memories of our interactions.

On another occasion, in the entrance lobby, I told them a fairy tale, beginning with "On the summit of a glass mountain, there was a golden castle. A prince and princess lived there. . . ."

At a later date, I related the same story to the former president of the Soviet Union, Mikhail Gorbachev, and his wife, Raisa Maximovna Gorbachev.

WIDER: What was the occasion?

IKEDA: It was in April 1993. Mr. Gorbachev, no longer Soviet president, was visiting Japan as he moved into new fields of activity. Though he had been endowed with absolute power as president of the Soviet Union, he was unafraid of losing his position and pursued democratic reform through a policy of perestroika[5] and played a leading role in bringing the Cold War to a conclusion. Throughout he had the support of his wife, Raisa.

After telling them the story, I said that they themselves were like the prince and princess who, while living on their hilltop and lacking nothing, descended into the wild turmoil below in order to save the unfortunate there. Silently nodding, Mr. Gorbachev said he accepted what I said as the words of a true friend. Reflecting on the years he had spent in a jungle of mistrust, suspicion, and prejudice, the years on the path of hardship he as a leader had chosen to follow, he expressed his firm resolution to join me in pioneering a new path to a better future. We later published a dialogue, *Moral Lessons of the Twentieth Century*, and we have continued to engage in dialogue up to the present.

WIDER: I am greatly impressed by your deeply trusting relation with Mr. Gorbachev and the way the two of you strive sincerely for the future of humanity. As a teacher and mother, I hope that our dialogue, too, can open a hopeful path to the future.

Sublime Motivations

IKEDA: A youth spent with the friendship of good books is fortunate and exalted. A close acquaintanceship with great literature both elevates and deepens our lives.

The nineteenth-century American Renaissance, when Emerson lived, was a period of many outstanding women writers. One of them was the famous Louisa May Alcott, author of *Little Women*, which has been beloved by both children and adults all over the world for more than 140 years. The book has been made into motion pictures numerous times, including several animated versions in Japan. I feel sure that it is one of your favorites, too.

WIDER: Louisa May Alcott is one of my favorite writers and women, and *Little Women* readily became a good friend early in my childhood. That interest stemmed directly from my mother. She had played the part of Jo in her high school's theatrical production and in turn shared her fascination with the book and its author. When my sister and I were still relatively young children, Mom read *Little Women* to us, a chapter each day as we ate lunch.

When I was a child, it was common for girls to play "Little Women." They would take on the different characters of the four daughters and pretend to be Amy, Jo, Beth, or Meg. My older sister, Susan, and I used to play these roles, too, but with just the two of us, we had to switch parts frequently. Our mother gave us Little Women dolls, and then we could play all the parts in turn.

IKEDA: Your mother wisely guided you into the world of stories. Learning this will be of great interest and use to the young mothers conducting a campaign to promote reading aloud to children in Japan.

My mentor used *Little Women*, Henrik Ibsen's *A Doll's House*, and Thomas Hardy's *Tess of the d'Urbervilles* as reading material in a young women's study group. At the time, Japan was just beginning to recover following the country's defeat in World War II, and life was still hard. Daily survival was as much as people could manage. Under such conditions, realizing that women would play a leading role in creating a century of peace, he wanted to provide them with the best spiritual nourishment available. He felt that he could encourage and cultivate young women by presenting to them the life story of Alcott, who brought her literary talents to fruition while supporting a poor family in times of great hardship.

I recall Toda's explanation that Alcott was able to compose works that so many found deeply moving and affecting precisely because, without collapsing under extraordinary difficulties, she strove tirelessly to become a better person. Josei Toda wanted all of the young women he taught to find happiness, and he was determined to make his wish a reality.

WIDER: Mr. Toda's choice bespeaks his deep understanding and far-reaching wisdom. In focusing on Louisa May Alcott, he gave young women a life of empowering strength—and a real life, not one romanticized or sheltered. This strength is often reflected in the female characters she created. Jo March is the most well known, and the Jo readers remember is the determined, aspiring, expressive person who would never be defeated.

Little Women remains popular in the United States to this day. My husband, daughter, and I just recently enjoyed an excellent musical production in Syracuse. And with a new documentary on Alcott's life airing on American television, *Little Women* will certainly continue to be prominently featured in bookstores.[1] Even when abridged or revised in updated language, the story survives well.

Orchard House in Concord, where the Alcotts lived, is one of the most visited places in the United States. Louisa May's fame attracts tourists from around the world.

IKEDA: Concord is of course famous for the battles at Lexington and Concord between British and colonial forces in April 1775 that started the American War of Independence. In my speeches, I have commended the good fight of Soka Gakkai International members engaged in grassroots movements for peace by referring to the actions of the anonymous heroes known as the Minutemen, youthful soldiers who fought on the front lines in the War of Independence.[2]

It was in Concord that writers and thinkers like Emerson, Thoreau, Hawthorne, and Alcott breathed fresh intellectual life into nineteenth-century America. Emerson, in particular, came to be known as the "sage of Concord." The region is thus doubly significant, not only as the home of the struggle for American political independence from England but also as the center of its spiritual and cultural independence.

Alcott wrote *Little Women* at Orchard House.[3] Coerced by poverty, her family changed residences nearly thirty times before finally settling down there for an extended period. Because of the property's many apple trees, of which her father was fond, Louisa

May referred to the house as "Apple Slump"—taken from the name of a dessert made from apples—a nickname I understand survives today.

Likening herself and her life to an apple, she once wrote:

> I think disappointment must be good for me, I get so much of it, and the constant thumping Fate gives me may be a mellowing process, so I shall be a ripe and sweet old pippin [apple] before I die.[4]

We can learn much from these moving, meaningful words. Our only option in life is to keep moving forward steadfastly and cheerfully, never succumbing to despair. Happiness comes to fruition only when we are strongly rooted in the soil of patience.

The Alcotts were close to the Emersons, weren't they? Emerson helped the Alcotts to find Orchard House.

WIDER: Yes, he did. Louisa May's father, Amos Bronson Alcott, had many ideas, most of which made no money. Louisa May's mother, Abigail May Alcott, was a pioneer in social work, which was absolutely crucial to societal well-being but not valued by society in monetary terms. Bronson was relentlessly idealistic, and Emerson, while often encouraging, could be vigorously skeptical of his activities. Still, generosity from the Emersons meant a great deal to the family.

Emerson's influence on Louisa May was large and multidimensional. She referred to him as her Goethe in that he was the intellectual invigorator of her ideas in the way that Johann Wolfgang Goethe had inspired the German novelist Bettine Brentano. Emerson was generous in his support, allowing Louisa May to borrow books from his study or letting her sister May, an aspiring artist, copy paintings he owned. He loved encouraging and helping young people, not just financially but in developing their own ideas.

IKEDA: As the word itself indicates, *encouragement* fills human hearts with courage. Emerson's support and magnanimity gave Alcott courage and hope, enabling her to develop her talents in spite of the hardships of her youth. In his study, she came into contact with the great works of Goethe, Shakespeare, Dickens, and others. Engaging in discussion with Emerson and his friends enabled her to imbibe the spirit of the American Renaissance, thus expanding and enriching her inner spiritual world.

I similarly want young people to read as many good books as possible; they provide spiritual nourishment and an intellectual foundation. I have loved reading since my youth and contributed to Soka University my collection of about seventy thousand publications. These included some I took with me for safekeeping into air-raid shelters during World War II and others that I used as texts when my mentor instructed me privately. I have memories associated with each and every book, and I donated them hoping to provide reading and study material for our students.

I presented another collection of about three thousand volumes to Soka University of America, when it opened in 2001. As founder, I am happy that these books will provide sustenance for students' futures.

THE BODHISATTVA WAY

WIDER: Your gifts bespeak a profound understanding of the role books may play in a student's life (students of any age, I might add). I think of Emerson's comment, "Many times the reading of a book has made the fortune of the man,—has decided his way of life."[5]

As you say, Louisa May Alcott was deeply influenced by Emerson, both through his personal character and through his thought. She played out a distinct version of self-reliance in her own life. She met her many difficulties with determination and without apology.

Emerson's ideas are included in various forms in her novels. For example, the heroine of *Work: A Story of Experience* starts out with untested idealism. She engages in many kinds of work and profits by the accompanying experience as she makes a life for herself. In the end, she develops a social services agency, where she can help other women stay employed. To borrow Emerson's words from his essay "Experience," she has accomplished the "true romance," "transform[ing] genius into practical power."[6] Alcott's book enjoyed considerable popularity when it was reprinted in the 1970s and '80s and deserves to be more widely read today.

IKEDA: No doubt. Undeniably, providing more fields in which women can be active would create avenues to employ the wisdom and sensitivity of women and build a better society. On this subject, Gorbachev commented to me that at present women generally are more active and more trusted than men—including in the world of politics. He also said that he feels the world would be a better place, and we would make fewer mistakes, if women had a greater voice in every area of society.

The heroine of *Work*, Christie Devon, reflects Alcott's ideas and is based on the author's experiences working desperately to support her family. I understand that Alcott's mother, Abigail, opened an employment agency for women like the one so vividly described in the book.

WIDER: Abigail, or Abby, focused on the kinds of social services that a community should provide in order to address and redress poverty. During the Civil War, Louisa May worked in the same vein and herself became a nurse. It was as powerful an experience for her as it was for Walt Whitman. She incorporated the experiences of the war and the feelings aroused in her by caring for wounded soldiers into *Hospital Sketches* as well as other stories. She also wanted her fiction to get people thinking hard about individual and societal choices.

IKEDA: She no doubt hoped the works written from her experiences would open people's eyes to the future and to social realities. For people with high ideals, even the most painful experiences or bitter memories can become priceless assets to encourage others. Alcott sublimated her sufferings into novels, revealing a pathway of courage and hope for others, especially women. In her noble life, we see the true brilliance of the human being.

Your moving description of her life reminds me of Mary Moody Emerson's encouragement to Emerson, "Scorn trifles, lift your aims; do what you are afraid to do; sublimity of character must come from sublimity of motive."[7] A great reader and woman of deep faith, Mary Moody Emerson certainly had a unique, powerful influence on Emerson's young life, guiding his reading and sending him letters filled with good advice (see Conversation Three).

WIDER: I am delighted at how highly you evaluate Mary. For a long time, her intellectual contributions were not taken seriously. Many people considered her an eccentric, if important, family member. Until Phyllis Cole's[8] and Nancy Simmons'[9] work, she was marginalized, when in fact she was an intellectual and spiritual heavyweight in her own right.

In her day, some people found her directness and honesty off-putting. Others delighted in it, because it kept them intellectually and spiritually honest. She was a mentor, certainly to the Emerson boys but also to many women who counted themselves lucky to converse with her, if not in person, then through correspondence. People looked forward to her letters, because she would always give them much to think about.

IKEDA: The light of the deep wisdom of life and the true brilliance of human nature are to be found in the lives of ordinary men and women striving earnestly to lead good lives.

When I conducted a dialogue with Ronald A. Bosco and Joel Myerson, both past presidents of the Thoreau Society, Emerson's "little-endians"[10] became a topic of conversation. Emerson used this term to describe human beings who, though not in the spotlight, are outstanding—and he named his aunt Mary among them.

Writing in his journal, Emerson emphasized the great worth of such individuals:

> The world looks poor & mean so long as I think only of its great men; most of them of spotted reputation. But when I remember how many obscure persons I myself have seen possessing gifts that excited wonder, speculation, & delight in me. . . .[11]

His words express the conviction underlying the SGI's many years of grassroots action for peace, culture, and education. It is always my desire to bring to light and honor as many of these anonymous, sincere, and great individuals as I can.

As Arnold J. Toynbee wisely said, history is ultimately defined not by what newspapers think makes good headlines but the deeper, slower movements.[12] In my understanding, he meant by the "deeper, slower movements" not the famous and celebrated but the countless heroes of the people who, aflame with a sense of mission, rise up and act.

WIDER: To paraphrase Mary Moody Emerson's words, sublime motivation yields sublime character. Here is wonderful encouragement for any person who might see himself or herself as just one inconsequential individual in a sea of billions. Worth is determined not by class, rank, or wealth but by the qualities that compose an individual's motivation.

What are that person's aspirations or larger understanding of purpose? What is an individual's source of insight? Does he or she see forward through to the implications of what is being undertaken? When a person acts from a firm commitment to justice, this work is worthwhile whether outwardly acknowledged or not.

Aunt Mary uses the word *sublime*. It remains a strong word to this day, but in her time, it carried special value. It suggested the grandeur and power of the greatest elements in nature—the Alps, Niagara Falls, Mount Fuji—and also the grandeur and power of the divine. The noble person is motivated by ideals strong enough to enable him or her to persevere under all circumstances, including injustice.

A person with *sublime motivations*, to borrow Mary Moody Emerson's phrase, essentially acts like a sun to others. Even if he or she suffers severe criticism and seemingly fails to move people, such a person often has a strong influence on later times. I find this decidedly heartening.

Real Partnership

IKEDA: In the long course of history, malicious criticism and slander cannot conceal the light of truth. From the viewpoint of the stern law of cause and effect, evil inevitably perishes and receives the harsh judgment of history.

Emerson associated with many dynamic women, including his aunt Mary and Louisa May Alcott, who shone like the sun for many people and who had unshakeable convictions enabling them to serve as pioneers of their day. Among them were Margaret Fuller, author of *Woman in the Nineteenth Century*, who exerted a strong influence on the women's rights movement, and Elizabeth Palmer Peabody, who made such great contributions to juvenile education as opening the first public kindergarten in the United States. The invigorating vitality of these women pioneered a new age.

WIDER: They were visionaries who worked for change in their own day and also wrote for the generations to come. In the 1870s, a concept called the "new woman" emerged in England and the United States. Essentially a working woman, the "new woman" was independent in economic, intellectual, and spiritual terms, and she was often criticized by people opposed to social change. Reading was a way of building community—whether reading *The Woman's Journal, The Independent*, or essayists like Emerson—and so reading was a strong source of encouragement for women who saw injustice in established society and sought to right wrongs, individually and collectively.

Emerson regarded women with respect for their particular potential and often showed intense concern about how society treated them and the societal constraints they faced. I have always liked the way Emerson used the word *equal* to mean having strength to accomplish things. He believed that human beings need to challenge themselves to be equal to the tasks confronting them. Those tasks were profoundly human and not to be limited by society's gendered norms.

While he lagged behind Margaret Fuller in openly criticizing the societal barriers that forbade women's direct political involvement, he nonetheless advocated for equal access to education as well as women's right to make decisions for themselves. He knew that women wanted to work productively and should have access to the employment they chose. He made this point—still revolutionary for its time—in an address titled "Woman," delivered at the Women's Rights Convention in Boston in 1855.

IKEDA: Yes, an undying address, in which he said: "Women are, by [conversation and] their social influence, the civilizers of mankind. What is civilization? I answer, the power of good women."[13] His brilliant view of civilization held that the power of conversation—the powerful voices of women awakened to their mission—is the driving force leading society and the epoch in the right direction.

Tsunesaburo Makiguchi and Josei Toda shared these high hopes for the positive influence of women, and they both did their utmost to bring it to full flower. For instance, more than a century ago, Mr. Makiguchi instituted a correspondence-education course for women. He was convinced that women were the builders of the ideal society of the future and would create peace. Soka Women's College, which you have visited twice to encourage students, carries on his educational dream.

After World War II, on the occasion of the founding of the Soka Gakkai's young women's division (July 19, 1951), Mr. Toda emphasized how important it was for young women to uphold the Buddhist philosophy of the dignity of life and become strong, self-reliant individuals. My wife, after her day's work at a bank, hurried to that inaugural meeting. Mr. Toda's teaching that all members deserve to become happy remains the starting point and guiding ideal of the young women's division to this day.

WIDER: Mr. Makiguchi and Mr. Toda chose to persevere in work they knew was going to be valuable instead of undertaking other work that would bring them status or fame. In this, they illustrate Emerson's idea of greatness, which he carefully distinguished from popular notions of eye-catching charisma or force-wielding power. When Emerson talked about what greatness was and what greatness does, he reminded his audiences "not to imitate or surpass a particular man in *his* way, but to bring out your own new way." He called greatness the "fulfillment of a natural tendency in each man" and opened its possibility to every human being. It was the "only platform on which all . . . can meet," precisely because all people carry within them their own contributing work.[14]

Emerson was always skeptical about work done for praise. For him, the work itself was the acclamation.

This makes me admire the Soka Gakkai all the more and your great founding leaders concerned with appreciating women and working for their happiness and well-being at a time when women's roles were limited, and women were treated as second-class citizens.

IKEDA: Adhering to the convictions of our first two presidents, I, too, have done all I could to create environments and educational systems enabling women to manifest their full potential. In addition, on every possible occasion, I have proclaimed the need to make ours a time of real partnership between the sexes.

WIDER: A transition to such a time is a major focal point of the twenty-first century. When I teach introductory women's studies at Colgate, I think about what makes true collaboration possible as well as the whole range of things that hold women back. Many of those obstacles are institutionalized, certainly in the workplace. Some are ingrained attitudes that create a severely limited understanding of women's capacity.

Even in this day, women are all too often characterized as "weak" or "lesser" or "dependent." The attitudes my mother had to endure in the 1950s and that women before her endured in their own place and time persist.

Worldwide, women's experiences are still silenced. Poverty disproportionately affects women, and women's capacity for productive work is poorly understood and often abused. War is countenanced in the name of terrorism, in the name of democracy, in the name of economic development or self-determination. The costs to women are unspeakably heavy. One need only think about the price women and girls have paid wherever war dominates. Such inequity, such inhumanity, must end.

The stories go on and on. How many girls are denied education or killed because they try to obtain it? There are so many situations where the free use of one's mind is not deemed important or is seen as "damaging" to what a girl or woman "should" be. How many girls with access to education are still tracked into certain areas and excluded from others?

Even with our guarantees from Title IX[15] in the United States, there are still many societal pressures or supports that steer women into certain fields of study but not others. Think how few women have real say in their healthcare and when or whether they give birth. And even something seemingly as trivial as taking a course in which there are no women writers on the syllabus or attending an art exhibition where there are no women artists sends a message about women's expendability.

No one should be taking a back seat to anyone. We should all be sitting together, listening, talking, and respecting the contributing work each person has to offer.

IKEDA: As early as the thirteenth century, Nichiren declared, "There should be no discrimination among those who propagate the five characters of Myoho-renge-kyo in the Latter Day of the Law, be they men or women."[16] Nichiren Buddhism encourages the establishment of a society in which gender discrimination and all other forms of discrimination have been transcended and the supreme dignity of life itself is allowed to shine forth. This doctrine shows how advanced Nichiren's philosophy was for the feudal Japanese society of his time.

Humanity's path forward must be one in which women's voices are heeded, and women are fully valued and respected. It is said that Mahatma Gandhi learned the spirit of nonviolence not from famous philosophers or religious scriptures but from his wife, Kasturba. Indeed, she supported him as a comrade in his nonviolence movement, joined in the resistance, and died in prison.

I remember chemist Linus Pauling, with whom I shared a dialogue, revealing that an important factor prompting him to take a stand against nuclear weapons was maintaining his wife's respect—"I felt compelled to earn and keep her respect."[17] When some Japanese women inquired how she felt about the interference and persecutions she and her husband had encountered, Ava

Helen Pauling replied that irresponsible, malicious people are to be found everywhere, and that the two of them would go on doing what they believed in.

To honor these two splendid couples at the opening of Soka University of America, one classroom building was named Mohandas and Kasturba Gandhi Hall and another Linus and Ava Helen Pauling Hall. On that occasion, Linus Pauling, Jr., recalled that his father felt his Nobel Peace Prize of 1962 should have been shared with his wife.

These two pairs of companions provide excellent models for an age of true partnership between the sexes. Naming the classroom buildings for them represents my hope as founder that the students who study there will bravely follow paths leading to a new peace and humanism.

A Return to Self-Reliance

IKEDA: A statement in Emerson's essay "Self-Reliance," which I loved reading as a young man, remains fixed in my memory: "Greatness appeals to the future."[1] This famous essay, which reflects the American Renaissance call for a revival of the human spirit, is still widely read today.

U.S. President Barack Obama listed it with Lincoln's writings and Gandhi's *An Autobiography: The Story of My Experiments with Truth* among the works he likes to read most. Many people seem to sense the vibrant presence of the philosophy of "Self-Reliance" in the young president's speeches.

WIDER: Emerson's words clearly strike fundamental notes for Mr. Obama. Hopefully the music Obama creates will be far more resonant with the health of the world soul than have been the dissonant militaristic policies in which the United States has been so heavily invested. When President Obama talks about *self-reliance*, it would seem to be Emersonian. While the term is often stripped of its Emersonian meaning, Mr. Obama returns it to its original definition. Rather than self-focused, isolated individuals,

Mr. Obama envisions a society in which each person works to his or her potential with the common commitment to the beautiful dignity of true relations.

IKEDA: For the creation of a new world, Emerson believed that each individual must be confident of his or her potential, and that all must work together to build a society in which these potentials can be fully realized. It is noteworthy that Emerson's philosophy of self-reliance remains current in the twenty-first century. Emerson argued that "repose" halts further development: "Power resides in the moment of transition from a past to a new state, in the shooting of the gulf, in the darting to an aim."[2]

Since September 2008, the financial crisis that caused confusion and uncertainty in global markets has dealt a major blow to the world economy. Many nations are still suffering the harsh aftermath of those events, and it has provoked a fundamental reevaluation of our societies' obsession with the unbalanced pursuit of material wealth. This crisis situation makes a reconsideration of Emersonian self-reliance all the more important. I am deeply convinced that if we turn our attention to the resource that is in fact closest at hand—the inner light of humanity—and set the human soul ablaze, we can generate the vital power needed to pioneer a new age.

WIDER: The great failure in the financial markets harshly reminds us of the poverty Wall Street inflicts. I don't want to minimize the economic hardships people are now experiencing and the devastation the collapse has been for those who could least afford it. At the same time, I look to this era as an opportunity for revisiting what gives true value to our lives.

A society whose prime motivator is consumption is by default a predatory society. What would it mean to become a society based on sharing and collaboration, rather than acquisition and competition? We have a long way to travel to realize this kind of society, and yet those working in the areas of true sustainability are showing us the way.

For many years now, people in the United States have measured success by possessions: the cars they own, the kind of house they live in, the things they can buy. A consumer-based society is undoubtedly dangerous: We are possessed by our possessions. Now seems like a particularly hopeful time in which we can think about our relationships with one another and with our communities. How do we share thoughts, hopes, dreams, work, common vision, and common goals?

The Occupy Movement continues to open possibilities independent of consumption. How are we taking care of and contributing to our communities? Have we lost community, this most vital aspect of human well-being? How do we measure life—by consumption and division? By appreciation and collaboration? What lasts beyond one individual life?

IKEDA: In January 2009 and 2010, in my annual peace proposals for SGI Day (January 26),[3] I discussed the dangers of capitalistic extremes. It is urgent for governments to take prompt steps to deal with economic recovery, poverty, and related issues. At the same time, there is a need to find ways to create a society in which the spirit of each individual can shine—a society characterized by deep spiritual fulfillment and the personal enrichment provided by strong interpersonal ties.

I have spoken on these issues with American futurologist Hazel Henderson, who courageously fights for environmental protection from a mother's viewpoint. Dr. Henderson emphasized that women pouring love and courage into the family and neighborhood have an important role in creating a "win-win era."[4]

WIDER: Her view speaks to the often-misunderstood possibilities in a mother's work. She is a public mentor.

My mother lived with a similar understanding. She believed strongly that everyone had a significant contribution to make, and that the home was central to nurturing such contributions. Having lived through the Great Depression of the 1930s, she intimately knew what it means to strive against the odds.

My mom read Emerson in high school and was strongly influenced by him. I recently found her high school notebooks containing her outline of "Self-Reliance." Here is what she wrote about his section on a "foolish consistency" being the "hobgoblin of little minds":

> Know your worth and be independent.
> Everyone has an equal chance to be great in his own way.
> 1. Take that chance and make the most of it
> 2. Do not try to mold your life after another.

In my mother's day, women's lives were all too often scripted into set patterns. Through her encounter with and interpretation of Emerson's ideas, I see her determination to act independently, to take chances, and to follow an ideal.

She set her sights on the best nursing school in the United States, persevering in her dream to become a nurse so that she could help a good friend who was seriously ill. She did just that: helped her friend to a much longer life and helped many others as well. These aspects of her life have been irreplaceable in shaping and supporting my own.

STELLAR MOMENTS

IKEDA: Your mother's noble aspirations and actions show a strong affinity to the bodhisattva way. I am moved by her unyielding conviction, which enabled her to realize her dream, and her beautiful spirit of friendship.

How did you first come into contact with Emerson's philosophy?

WIDER: Like Mom, I was influenced by my grandmother, who loved reading Emerson. She admired his philosophy from an early age and gave her high-school commencement address on "Self-Reliance." When I was eighteen, we all took a trip to Concord. It was a beautiful fall day; the trees were a splendid gold. This was my first visit both to Emerson's house and to the Old Manse, where he wrote "Nature." It was an important factor in deepening my interest in him.

Then, several years later, I chose Emerson research as my own work, thanks largely to a marvelous seminar I had taken during college with two extraordinary professors, thinkers, activists: Paul Schmidt and Gail Baker. Mom was delighted that I decided to focus on Emerson, because his ideas mattered greatly to her, as they did to her mother. I remember sharing everything I was thinking about Emerson with Mom and her enthusiasm about the things I was learning.

IKEDA: Emerson's thought transcended time to connect three generations—grandmother, mother, and daughter—in a beautiful spiritual bond.

My mentor always urged us to face life confidently and be true to ourselves. This was in the turbulent years immediately following World War II, when society was shrouded by uncertainty, and people could think of little more than their day-to-day survival. In these conditions, President Toda taught ordinary people the importance of living powerfully for a mission with the courage and hope fostered through Buddhist practice.

The dramatically deteriorating economic situation imperiled his business enterprises. I alone gave him unfailing support and protection. Once, as we shared a simple lunch, looking straight into my eyes, President Toda said: "Daisaku, in life, the final triumph is true victory. The wins and losses of youth are not the last word. They are only training for the ultimate, final victory." These words are engraved in my heart.

WIDER: I, too, have long treasured certain words. I have in mind a note my mother wrote and gave me on November 23, 1975. I was a sophomore in high school, and my sister, then in college and majoring in French and music, was studying in France. It was the first time she had been away for a long period and our first Thanksgiving without her. Mom, believing my sister might be homesick, wrote her long letters about what was happening at home. Especially at the holiday, she had been thinking about what to send to Susan as encouragement, and her own thoughts came to her in the form of the words "A grateful heart is a happy heart." She wrote them in her letter to Susan and in the note she gave me.

Susan and I loved the Thanksgiving holiday from the time we were small children—watching the Macy's Thanksgiving Day Parade on television, luxuriating in our time off from school, performing the wonderful stories Susan invented for our dolls. For me, these days were filled with the spirit of gratitude and thankfulness.

At this particular Thanksgiving, Mother had been missing my sister and probably had been lamenting the way time brings distance. Lives change so that we can't always be together, and yet we could still find reason for thanks. She may have hoped her words would stay with me for a long time to come. They certainly have. They remain important to me to this day as I reflect on them, many years after my parents' deaths. Our loved ones stay with us in such a good way through the gratitude we share.

IKEDA: It's a beautiful, heart-warming story of a wonderful family that should be transmitted to generations to come. "A grateful heart is a happy heart." What golden words of loving attentiveness and the true wisdom of life! Though simple, they express one of life's most important truths and convey your mother's profound love and wisdom.

We all have such decisive, illuminated moments in our lives. The Austrian writer Stefan Zweig called them *Sternstunden der Menschheit*—rare but highly dramatic moments in the life of an individual or a society that exert a defining influence. They are like stars steadily illuminating the shifting darkness. For you, the memory of this shared time with your mother as a high-school student was one of these stellar moments.

WIDER: "Stellar moments" is a beautiful, lyrical way of describing such experiences, and I will be all the more mindful of such times as I look to the stars in the clarity of a vibrant night sky.

Especially when things aren't going well, there's nothing like this saying of my mother's to put things in a much better perspective. Most recently, it has been tremendously important whenever I suffer migraines. There are times when pain keeps me from working or reading. Even thought changes. It helps to rest my mind in thankfulness.

When I see something beautiful, I think, "Oh, I wish I could say thank you to the person who created it." This sense of appreciation definitely comes from the early stages of my life, when gratitude was the very air I breathed. It was my mother's greatest gift to me.

There are wonders all around us. Will we see and affirm them? If we lack a vital and healthy sense of appreciation for wonder, we are likely to act by way of negation. With appreciation, we affirm. From the energy appreciation generates, we see the way to build, transform, create, contribute. This is amazing.

IKEDA: I am deeply moved by and wholeheartedly convinced of what you say. Buddhism teaches that gratitude is extremely important. The grateful person is pure-hearted and beautiful, shining with nobility.

Many intellectuals from all over the world with whom I have met fit this description. For instance, the world-famous English violinist Yehudi Menuhin had a grateful heart. I remember vividly how, when we met in Tokyo some years ago, he was careful to thank and bow politely to everyone who did anything for him. During our talks, he told me quite frankly:

> [With age,] one certainly acquires knowledge about a wide range of things. However, it seems to me that in many cases this knowledge in fact becomes a barrier that blocks such natural human responses as sympathy and encouragement.[5]

In modern society, there is a lamentable tendency for people to think only of themselves, to manipulate, exploit, and take advantage of others with shameless arrogance. Such self-centered, ungrateful behavior and inability to appreciate others ultimately leads to a sad, lonely life.

Gratitude to the parents who rear us is a fundamental principle of humanity, which is the duty of a sound education to teach. Whenever I visit Soka University or the Soka Junior and Senior High Schools, I urge the students to honor and be good to their parents. To be truly learned means you don't cause your father to worry or bring to your mother sorrow. You are not fully educated if you have no sense of gratitude for your parents and are not filial. Only people who always treat those around them with gratitude and consideration can lead rich lives and help make society more humane and caring.

By way of encouraging young educators, Arnold J. Toynbee said he hoped they would try to create a society in which people say "thank you" to one another more often today than they did yesterday. Surely the world would be a much more peaceful place if everyone would sincerely say "thank you" to wonderful mothers like your own.

WIDER: It is sad that in the United States, true respect often goes wanting. For example, mothers have so much at stake in bearing and raising children. Not only do they have a powerful responsibility to and for their children, but their own lives are profoundly changed. In part, such change has been artificially imposed, fabricated by societal constraints. While lip-service praise has been paid to them, and they've been put up on pedestals, mothers haven't been respected as human beings with vastly interesting, creative potential, who will, or should, find free and welcome expression.

I'm especially moved by a passage from your poem "A Mother's Victory Is True Victory":

> No one in the world is a match for a mother.
> A person may hold office or stand in a position of power,
> but no one ranks above a mother.
> Compared with the love and compassion of a mother,
> honors fade away and medals cease to shine.

Your poem reminds us how corrosive societal values can be. A fixation with position and accomplishment blinds us to the real power of compassion and love. We need to remember that, no matter what our age, we're children. We all come from our mothers. There is no point in life where we are not still a child in some substantial way. There are always mothers in our midst, and we are their children. A world that forgets its mothers is a wasteland.

IMPERFECTION

IKEDA: The tendency you describe has parallels in Japan, too. Mothers, who bring new life into the world and then protect and foster these new lives with love, are the foundation for all of society.

A society that fails to have gratitude for these noble beings does not have a bright future. I have written numerous poems in praise of mothers because of my wish to offer sincere encouragement to mothers, carrying out the world's noblest work, day after day.

When the celebrated historian Eric Hobsbawm was asked to name the person he considered most symbolic of the twentieth century, he said mothers, because they are most common, wherever on the face of the Earth they may live.[6] I believe that by "common" he didn't mean simply ordinary, rather that mothers embody the quality of true humanity most fully, representing the wisest, most dependable, most wholesome, and most humane qualities that we have. Once, when a business leader asked whom I considered the greatest person in the world, I replied that mothers are the greatest of all.

WIDER: This understanding of "common" aptly defines an ideal we should all explore. Rather than privileging the exceptional or uncommon, we must reevaluate what deepens a person's humanity. This is why we must build a society that fully appreciates mothers, creating communities in which a mother's humanity is nourished and supported in its fullest sense. To do this, we must learn from the kind of encouragement so essential to your work.

I know how wearying the raising of a child can be. One's physical, intellectual, and emotional strengths are exercised in ever new ways. The early years of a child's life are especially demanding for a mother physically, as she adjusts to different rhythms of sleep and to the child's own vigorous and expansive energy.

It is sad that, in the United States as in many other cultures, an innate hostility to mothers appears in the standard of perfection to which they are held. Imperfection is elemental to all life, to all human relationships. There must be this dynamism, so that individuals can be free to learn, to take risks, to respect the ever-changing manifestations of existence.

IKEDA: Many of the readers of this dialogue are mothers with small children. I am sure that your words will deeply encourage large numbers of them and take a load off their minds.

Nichiren compares the compassion of the Buddha striving to save living beings to the compassion of a mother feeding her infant child.[7] Such compassion arises naturally; it is "originally inherent and not created."[8] In other words, it is not coming from a societal demand that mothers live up to some standard of perfection but from the natural expression of life itself.

I believe that when children grow up, they remember not their mothers' mistakes but the deep love and the warm, selfless care they provided. As Romain Rolland, one of my favorite writers, wrote of his mother: "She made me. Not only on the day of my birth; but to the day of her death, she nourished the life within me."[9]

To the mothers who gave them life, even the greatest philosophers, politicians, and educators are always their little children. As long as a tree is firmly rooted, it can rise tall and strong, adding rings of growth with each passing year. A mother's love is like the tree's deep roots, spreading and continuing to nourish her children even after they grow up and move away.

WIDER: In this respect, too, as long as parent and child understand each other, perfection in daily events is unnecessary. Another thing I would say is that there is strength in numbers. I think mothers oftentimes end up feeling isolated or being isolated, because they have children to attend to and lack opportunities to make friends or to maintain these life-affirming friendships outside the home.

Thinking of this reminds me of Ruth Haskins Emerson and the way she devoted an hour every day to devotional reading, and the way the family respected her time, as we mentioned before (see Conversation Three). In all probability, it was a practice she brought with her to marriage. She also was strong in her friendships with many women.

IKEDA: I can see why Emerson and his brothers had the greatest respect for their mother, Ruth. Like Mrs. Emerson, Margarita Vorobyova-Desyatovskaya of the Russian Academy of Sciences, a friend of mine and a leading researcher on the Lotus Sutra, was widowed at a young age. But, triumphing over her sorrow, Dr. Vorobyova-Desyatovskaya raised fine children and achieved much in the scholarly field she chose as her mission in life. Specializing in the Lotus Sutra, the paramount scripture of Mahayana Buddhism, she has derived spiritual support from its admonition to have faith in our own strength. As she put it:

> If you accept the teachings of the Lotus Sutra, even unexpected setbacks or misfortunes won't discourage you or frighten you. You know that the sun will rise again tomorrow and a new day will dawn. You know that if you smile at others, they will smile back at you.[10]

Despite her usual calm demeanor, her voice resounded with strong conviction when she said this. As Nichiren wrote, "Winter always turns to spring."[11] I want to transmit these hope-giving words to hard-working mothers all over the world.

CONVERSATION SEVEN

The Rhythms of Nature

IKEDA: Spring is the season of hope, vibrant activity, and fresh beginnings. In Japan, schools and companies begin a new year in April. I am always filled with joy when I see the cherry trees in bloom and the new students sparkling with life on the campuses of Soka Junior and Senior High Schools and Soka University. Watching bright, talented young people forging friendships as they grow and develop together reminds me of a profoundly moving passage in Goethe's poem "On the New Year":

> But, on us gently
> Shineth a true one [friendship],
> And to the new one
> We, too, are new.[1]

WIDER: Beautiful words. At Colgate, our spring semester begins in January, in the heart of winter. Over the next four months, the season slowly shifts from the mind-tingling cold of a midwinter morning to the soft light of an early spring afternoon. In upstate New York, spring is a good model for us all. It takes its time. Spring arrives in a slight change of light here, the shift in a bird's voice, snow moving from daily presence to occasional companion, finally revealing open ground, and then our first flowers appear, appropriately called snowdrops (Galanthus). This is spring: the slight differences that betoken and herald the vigor of life readying to return.

IKEDA: You put it beautifully and poetically. Emerson and Thoreau also frequently expressed their love of spring in their writings.

> The first sparrow of spring! The year beginning with younger hope than ever! The faint silvery warblings heard over the partially bare and moist fields from the blue-bird, the song-sparrow, and the red-wing.[2]

This is from Thoreau's *Walden*. How vividly the refined soul of the poet communicates the rhythms of nature. When one reads it aloud, one can smell the fragrance of new grass and hear the singing of birds.

WIDER: A poet is one who hears nature's rhythms and opens the ears of others. Thoreau's words write the music he heard everywhere in the natural world: music for the ear, the eye, the spirit.

IKEDA: At the age of seventeen, the youthful Emerson wrote:

> Spring has returned and has begun to unfold her beautiful array, to throw herself on wild-flower couches, to walk abroad on the hills and summon her songsters to do her sweet homage.[3]

The "songsters" are, of course, the birds that Thoreau so loved, too. The scene Emerson describes certainly resonates with his youthful spirit.

Elsewhere in his journals, Emerson recorded the words of his son: "The flowers talk when the wind blows over them."⁴ Emerson was thirty-seven and little Waldo four at the time. Possibly, the boy made this remark when the two were out walking and talking together. Nature can cultivate a richly poetic spirit in young lives. Emerson also wrote: "Ah, Nature! The very look of the woods is heroical and stimulating."⁵ The woods and nature as a whole are brimming with the energy of life, enfolding and nurturing our spirits.

Adults must ensure that children are given the opportunity to grow and develop freely by coming into contact with the natural environment. Those who have the chance to experience the full richness of nature as children are indeed fortunate.

Earlier in our dialogue, you mentioned your sun-drenched home in New Mexico (see Conversation One). What natural features remain especially vivid in your mind?

WIDER: The mountains. In Albuquerque, you can always see mountains. To the east of the city are the Sandia and Manzano Mountains, constant presences, and to the west, one can see the mountain called Tsoodzil ("Blue Bead," or "Turquoise") in Navajo or Kaweshtima ("Place of Snow") by those at Acoma Pueblo (I prefer not to use the American name, coming as it does from a military history). When I was very young, and Albuquerque was much smaller, you could even see north to the Jemez Mountains.

I've often thought that being able to see across such distances, land rising to mountain, mountain to sky, helped me develop a certain expansiveness of mind. Ideas have room to unfold because even the physical boundaries of mountains lead straight to limitless sky. I love the complementary colors of the sky's resonant shades of blue and the mountains' ranging spectrum of reds, blues, and sun-washed golds. I've frequently wished you could come to New Mexico because, as your nature photographs show, you would love the myriad colors.

In "Nature," Emerson wrote, "We are never tired, so long as we can see far enough."[6] In such a clarifying, pure-lighted expanse, our spirits rise to meet the mountains and fill with the energy of that full, yet open, distance.

IKEDA: With a history of more than three centuries, Albuquerque is known for being older than the United States itself. It is located on a high plain at the confluence of several branches of great southward-flowing rivers that flow from the Rocky Mountains.

Many SGI members reside in Albuquerque and throughout New Mexico, where they are contributing to their communities. I feel a wonderful serendipity in the fact that you are a native of the city. It inspires me to redouble my prayers for the continued development of the city of Albuquerque and the state of New Mexico, as well as my efforts for its friendly relations with Japan.

I saw the magnificent Rocky Mountains in 1996, when I visited the University of Denver in Colorado, Albuquerque's neighbor to the north. I shall never forget the majestic natural drama of the faintly visible moon rising in the sunlit blue sky over snow-capped peaks.

Mountains have the power to forge character. In 1995, I viewed the Himalayas with Nepalese village children and told them:

> Shakyamuni Buddha grew up in sight of the Himalayas.
> He strove to grow up to be like these mountains—to be a
> bold and towering victor in life. You can do the same. You
> live in a wonderful place, and I am sure you'll all become
> great human beings.

I can still see the light shining in their beautiful eyes as they smiled and nodded to me.

President Makiguchi, an outstanding geographer, wrote of the uplifting effect that mountains have:

It is natural that mountains have an especially close relationship to our lives. Whenever we look up, the mountains are there: an integral part of our world, friends.... Their presence grows within our minds and deeply affects our lives and personalities, unconsciously.[7]

WIDER: Mr. Makiguchi's profound and meaningful words inspire me always to keep the mountains present, even when physical distance separates me from them. I am also reminded of a beautiful connection in the Navajo language, where the word for *mountain* and the word for *strength* are closely related.

As poet Luci Tapahonso writes:

We understand that we are surrounded by mountains, dziil,
and thus that we are made of strength, dziil, nihi nihidziil.
We are strong ourselves. We are surrounded by mountains
that help us negotiate our daily lives.[8]

I wonder if there is also such a connection in the Japanese language. What kinds of places does Mrs. Ikeda find most strengthening?

IKEDA: In Japan, mountains are often seen as symbolizing desirable character traits. For example, the celebrated novelist Eiji Yoshikawa wrote that, instead of fretting over becoming this or that, people should strive to be like Mount Fuji, silent and immovable.

Many of the Chinese characters that contain the radical "mountain" imply character traits, with such meanings as "to be noble and exalted," "to stand bravely," and "to be lofty and dignified." As a matter of fact, my wife's name, Kaneko, is written with characters meaning "lofty peak," which also contain the radical "mountain." Josei Toda bestowed the characters on her when we married. Her father and mother came from Gifu, a part of Japan known for its forests and mountains, and sent my wife there as a child for safety during World War II.

In reply to your question about what kinds of places are special to my wife, she once told me that Mr. Toda had given her this verse: "May your gentle image in the moonlight / be filled with the strength of the Mystic Law."[9] She said that the sentiment behind the verse inspired her to never give in, no matter what happened. This is why I think perhaps she is more strengthened by the mentor-disciple bond than by any specific place or topography.

Buddhism teaches that wherever we are is inherently the "Land of Eternally Tranquil Light that has existed for all time."[10] In other words, wherever one lives becomes the best of all possible places through one's practice of Buddhism.

My wife often says that hearing how our precious Soka Gakkai comrades have overcome hardships to find great joy makes her happier than anything else. She and I pray daily that all of these precious members will win a life of enduring happiness, and we spend every possible moment encouraging each of them.

As Mr. Toda's verse says, unless we possess both gentleness and strength, we can't become "mountains" imparting courage and peace of mind. These are especially important qualities for leaders to have, I believe.

TO SEE TRULY

WIDER: One of the reasons I became interested in Emerson was his lifelong fascination with the ways nature and spirit are intertwined. As I have said before, I was also influenced by my mother and grandmother (see Conversation Four). I only started studying Emerson formally during college. I took an introductory course in American literature and still have the book from that class. I recently looked into it to see what I had underlined, so I could find out what had spoken to me thirty years ago. It was clear that at the time (I was nineteen years old), I was very interested in the connection between nature and spirit.

Another area of particular interest was Emerson's emphasis on what it means to "see truly." We all have eyes, but do we see? Do our casual glances lead to insight? Emerson calls his readers to be "seers"—people of deep insight and foresight.

In English, the words *see* and *seer* are so closely related that it would appear easy to become such a person, but as we all know, there has been little encouragement for such seers. And yet, Emerson suggests, this potential lives within every person.

IKEDA: He contemplated important philosophical themes with his keen, youthful vision.

Buddhism teaches that the act of seeing is inseparable from the beholder's life condition. As the scriptures explain, "Hungry spirits see the waters of the [the Ganges] river as fire, human beings see them as water, and heavenly beings see them as amrita [a sweet beverage said to give immortality]."[11] The waters are the same in all cases, but each type of being sees them differently in accord with its own state.

This is why it's so important to polish our lives to the brightness of a clear mirror. It enables us to reflect the beauty and richness of the world, as well as the true nature of things, clearly in our minds.

I imagine that experiences in college further strengthened your interest in Emerson.

WIDER: When I got to graduate school, I was going to study Nathaniel Hawthorne. But the Hawthorne professor made it clear that we were going to have to study his way. While I liked his way of studying Hawthorne, his inflexible approach made me nervous.

He also offered an Emerson seminar. My Emerson and Thoreau seminar had been a highpoint in my undergraduate education, and I was glad to return to reading Emerson. It was during this graduate seminar that I decided to study Emerson in depth. I realized that, as much as Emerson had been studied, there was so much that had not been discussed. At the time, his sermons were still unpublished, as were his later lectures, poetry, and topical notebooks.

I had always been interested in the connection between religion and literature, and wanted to see what he continued to work on from the early days of his career and what he discarded. I wondered if critics were right in saying that it was all left behind after he left the pulpit. My professor suggested that I take a look at the unpublished sermons that were kept at the Houghton Library, Harvard's rare book and manuscript library. My first visit was short— less than a week—but enough time to formulate the heart of my dissertation project on *The Sermons*.

IKEDA: Emerson entered the Theology Department at Harvard and eventually became a preacher. However, concluding that religion should not just be empty ritual but something one practices— a person's lifeblood, rationale, and bedrock—he quit his ministerial career at the age of twenty-nine. As we discussed earlier, Emerson's views on religion and faith are relevant to us today (see Conversation Three).

Emerson's father died when Emerson was only eight, leaving the family in financial straits. As a result, he did not have the opportunity for the unlimited study that his fellow students enjoyed. In order to help his mother, struggling to raise her family after her husband's death, Emerson lived at the college president's house and served as his freshman helper to defray schooling costs. His youth was not an easy one. In spite of these many hardships, he strove diligently, winning essay competitions and being selected as the poet of his graduating class.

The hardships of youth become life's treasure. My mentor also faced great adversity in his youth, as did his mentor, Tsunesaburo

Makiguchi. In his youth, an eagerness to learn inspired Makiguchi to leave his hometown for the northern island of Hokkaido, where he worked as an errand boy at the Otaru police office while attending night school. Though he spent his days serving tea, running errands, filing documents, and cleaning up, he refused to let this fatiguing work get him down and always found time to read books and study. He was so devoted to his studies that the others in the office called him "the Studious Errand Boy."

WIDER: I stop and think about how hard that must have been. Envisioning his enduring spirit and unwavering persistence, I can imagine how he persevered in his love of learning despite those time-taking, wearying tasks.

Your words impress me with the undeniable truth that great hardships in one's youth often become the means for growth and development. We see this again and again in history.

Unfortunately, in our increasingly fast-paced, individual-centered world, it can be difficult to see through time and feel a strong connection with those who have gone before us and with those yet to come. In such isolation, it can also be difficult for young people to comprehend the power and potential of their own abilities. It is all too easy to sell oneself short and settle for less than what one can do.

Here is where it is so helpful, perhaps even crucial, to come into contact with something profoundly inspiring. For example, listening to the students at Soka University speak of the meaningful time they spent visiting the Emerson house in Concord, I clearly saw the deep connection they felt and the profound feeling of renewed dedication they experienced.

IKEDA: Studying the lives of great people of all times and places can have an eye-opening effect on young students. This is why both Soka University of Japan and Soka University of America have treasured collections of great individuals' memorabilia. Among them are a letter from Emerson to Thoreau and autographed manuscripts from Walt Whitman and Henry Wadsworth Longfellow.

Emerson was busy lecturing and writing toward the end of 1855, the date of the letter in our collection. Written while he was traveling, it asks Thoreau to proofread one of his manuscripts.[12] Emerson and Thoreau were bound by strong, deep ties of mutual trust and respect. I hope that students at Soka University of Japan and Soka University of America will learn from the spirit of these two towering figures as they dedicate their lives to working for the betterment of society and world peace.

CONVERSATION EIGHT

Sympathy and Likeness

IKEDA: Good books enlarge the universe of the spirit. As Thoreau wrote in a famous passage from *Walden*, "Books are the treasured wealth of the world and the fit inheritance of generations and nations."[1] In his youth, Thoreau learned from and was greatly inspired by Emerson. He absorbed much knowledge from the large collection of books in Emerson's study and appears to have read many books about Asian philosophy and religion. The notes he made from his readings extend to more than five thousand pages. Reading can indeed be a bright mirror for self-improvement.

> *Reading shines like gold.*
> *It is the wellspring of triumph,*
> *It is the helpful companion to happiness,*
> *the path leading to the great.*
> *Reading good books and*
> *attacking bad books*
> *make you people of justice.*

I once wrote these lines for the Soka University of Japan students. They are displayed in the central library, serving as encouragement to read.

WIDER: Each word and phrase conveys your deeply compassionate affection for the students as well as your boundless expectations for them. Nurturing a love for reading and fostering delight in beautifully thought-provoking books have long been important to me, particularly for the younger generation but also for readers of all ages.

IKEDA: For several years, young people's disinclination to read was a serious concern in Japan, but more recently the number of children who enjoy reading has started to increase. The *Mainichi Shimbun,* one of the major Japanese newspapers, conducts an annual survey of student reading habits. In 2009, their report showed that more than 70 percent of junior-high and high-school students liked reading books. This was a ten-point increase over 2002.

It seems likely that the increase results from reading-promotion campaigns in schools throughout the country. Still, the number of books read monthly by children who say they love reading decreases as they grow older. Whereas 75 percent of elementary-school readers read more than five books a month, the figure drops to 55 percent for middle-school students and still further to 24 percent for high-school students. The problem now is how to keep reading habits acquired in elementary school deeply rooted as children grow.

WIDER: Encouraging an interest in reading is also a major challenge in America. At my own university, I see students who have become so trained to read only for the test that they no longer read for pleasure or intellectual stimulation. Often they feel they have no time for such reading—the "creative reading" Emerson described in "The American Scholar."[2]

A white paper issued by the U.S. government in 2004 warned that ours is a nation at risk because reading is at risk. Reading has been compromised in an age overwhelmed by information. Surveys show that fewer and fewer people read literary works like poetry, novels, plays, or tales.

To counter the trend, programs have been created to encourage reading, for example, P.A.R.P. (Parents as Reading Partners) in public elementary schools and "The Big Read," sponsored by the National Endowment for the Arts. This program reaches older readers, working through four hundred regional organizations, including libraries and museums. Each community decides to discuss a book that is of particular interest and local pertinence. The idea is to make reading not just an individual action but a communal activity.

IKEDA: Selecting books of local interest is an excellent idea. This "Big Read" program is well received because it promotes reading and also strengthens communication and community solidarity. In *A Geography of Human Life,* Tsunesaburo Makiguchi had this to say on the importance of the local community in the cultivation of the mind:

> Family, friends, neighbors, and community groups can nurture us in so many ways. This immediate, direct experience available to us through the natural and social environments of our homelands can foster compassion, goodwill, friendship, kindness, sincerity, and humble hearts.[3]

It is important for people to work together to improve education at the community level through such efforts as promoting reading.

In Japan, in 2005, a resolution was passed to promote an environment in which all Japanese citizens, in every area and at every stage of life, had equal access to the rich culture of the written word. In response to this, in the same year, Soka University started an institution-wide reading movement called the Soka Book Wave.[4]

The Soka University library has more than a million books. One of the aims of the new movement was to enhance student access to the collection while making it possible for students' parents, correspondence-course students, graduates, and local community members to borrow books, based on the belief that libraries are a bastion for lifelong education.

In November 2009, the university held conferences and public lectures on the culture of the written word. These were held in connection with the designation of 2010 as the National Year of Reading by parliamentary resolution in Japan.

WIDER: The Soka Book Wave creates a powerful opportunity for connection. Ease of accessibility is key, as is encouraging a type of reading that develops empathy.

Currently in the United States, the emphasis in reading seems to be on extraction: You get something out of the words, as if you were removing a purchased item from its packaging. This consumer-based model shows up in popular reading choices. We read "how-to" guides and "self-help" manuals. While there is a place for these, their focus on particular methods and on self-involvement limits the imaginative capacity for empathy.

Even the ever-popular stories about celebrities—whether sports, Hollywood, or political figures—are troubling because they often encourage a kind of voyeuristic and judgmental stance. Fiction, poetry, plays ask us to engage far more expansively.

A favorite writer of mine, Simon Ortiz, puts it this way: "Without this sharing in the intellectual, emotional, physical, and spiritual activity, nothing much happens."[5] This line of thought reminds me of the conversations I had with junior-high and high-school students at the Soka schools, because they were thinking exactly the same kind of thing.

THEIR SPIRITS REMAIN

IKEDA: As founder of these schools, I take the greatest joy in what you say. At the Soka Junior and Senior High Schools, we strive to create an environment in which pupils can become familiar with good books. In 2008, wishing to be part of the program, I wrote an article for the *Seikyo Shimbun* newspaper[6] titled "On Dante—in Tribute to the Century of Youth," intended for schoolchildren. I also delivered a series of lectures on "Goethe—the Man" at Soka University and on Maupassant's *A Woman's Life* at Soka Women's College, exploring the themes of learning, life, and happiness.

In the Dante article, while explaining how his youthful reading and study at the University of Bologna laid the foundation for Dante's character formation and literary life, I said:

> Learning makes a person stronger. It enriches their life. I hope all of you will grow up to be the kind of leader who empathizes with the suffering and who comes to the aid of the unfortunate. To do that, you must study now. The mission of the Soka Junior and Senior High Schools is to train great leaders of world peace.

I fondly remember touring the restored Casa di Dante, when I visited Florence in June 1981. A stern bust of the poet was inset in the exterior wall of the stone house on a busy corner; Dante's visage was that of a warrior who has struggled indomitably all his life.

I have indelible memories of visiting numerous places like the

Dante house and other sites associated with the great spirits of human history during my travels to meet and speak with world leaders and encourage our overseas members.

WIDER: Visiting places associated with the great authors of good books is certainly a deeply moving experience. My visits to the Emerson house have inspired me in many ways. While many years have passed since Emerson lived with his family and friends in this place, the years disappear in the physical space of the home. Upstairs in the children's room, you can see the dollhouse (or "baby house," as it was called) with which his daughters Ellen and Edith played and the rocking horse beloved by all the children. Downstairs, Emerson's hat and walking sticks remain just where they would have been, so he could select his and offer one to his companion as they headed off to walk—the outdoors always the best "room" for study.

For his indoor study, there is the unforgettable bookshelf-lined room with a painting by May Alcott and his prized copy of the painting "The Three Fates."[7] An Aeolian harp poised on the windowsill brings in the ethereal music Emerson loved. And in the center of the room, there is the sturdy, circular desk where Emerson struggled with his energy-filled sentences.

IKEDA: One must appreciate the efforts the people who care for the place expend in transmitting his noble life and thought. I also agree that the outdoors is always the best "room" for study. No doubt Emerson was able to spread the wings of his intellect and imagination as he strolled through nature, pondering deep thoughts, conversing with friends, and enjoying a profound sense of oneness with the natural world.

As a young man I, too, often sought out quiet places outdoors to read. I remember using three golden gingko leaves as a bookmark in my copy of *Leaves of Grass* in the autumn immediately after World War II.

I visited Whitman's house in Long Island, New York, in 1981 and was moved by the many precious manuscripts there, including a letter of commendation that Emerson wrote for *Leaves of Grass,* which was not well received when it was first published. I also met some of the volunteers of the Birthplace Association and asked them several questions, such as what they thought Whitman's best poem was, what the illness he died of was, what his reputation was in his time, and so on, all of which they graciously answered.

This humble dwelling of the great poet, I said to them, imparts to countless people incomparably greater value than any giant structure could, and I expressed my sincere respect and appreciation to them for cherishing Whitman, transmitting his spirit, and maintaining the house so filled with his presence.

WIDER: In conversation with my students, I often talk about how meaning belongs so powerfully to certain places. Where people have lived full, creative, generous lives, their spirits remain. If we are attentive, we will honor the creativity and courage that once spoke from within this place. But we must truly "attend": be present through our keen and thought-filled learning, wholeheartedly listening to the voices that echo through the years, so that we might understand our part in the ongoing dialogue.

SUNRISE WITHIN

IKEDA: When I visited Goethe's home in Frankfurt, I felt the commitment of the Frankfurt citizens dedicated to eternally transmitting the "voices that echo through the years," as you put it, at Goethe's birthplace. Though destroyed in World War II, the splendid five-story building has been restored by the Goethe

Foundation. I understand that bricks from the original building have been used in the front wall.

In 2009, I met with Dr. Manfred Osten, advisor to the Goethe Society in Weimar, and discussed the importance of carrying on Goethe's thought and spirit. On that occasion, the society presented me with its Goethe Medal, one of only twelve that Goethe personally commissioned (in 1816).

In 1981, I visited Leo Tolstoy's house and museum in Moscow, and in 2008, I had an opportunity to meet Tolstoy's great-great-grandson Vladimir Tolstoy, curator of the Tolstoy Estate Museum at Yasnaya Polyana, Tolstoy's birthplace. In 1994, Mr. Tolstoy left a successful career in journalism to return to the Tolstoy home and work for the preservation and continuation of his great-great-grandfather's literary and philosophical legacy. I was impressed by his choice, reflecting the highest personal convictions.

When and how did you and your colleagues found the Ralph Waldo Emerson Society?

WIDER: The Emerson Society is still quite recent, founded in 1989 by a group of like-minded colleagues at the Modern Language Association annual conference. Formed to bring together people interested in studying Emerson, we are a group of professors, although we do have a goodly number of members from other walks of life.

An interesting side note: The Thoreau Society began much earlier, in 1941. There is great irony here since Thoreau is better known for leaving societal organizations than for joining them.

As for activities, the Emerson Society always holds two sessions at the American Literature Association Conference every year and a session at the Thoreau Society annual gathering so that aspects of Emerson's work can be featured and discussed. One of the big projects that the society first worked on was the celebration of the bicentennial of Emerson's birth, which required much energy but attracted much interest as well.

IKEDA: I talked about the 2003 bicentennial celebration with Ronald A. Bosco and Joel Myerson of the Thoreau Society. In addition to being joint chairmen on that occasion, they have each served as president of the Emerson Society. This suggests that the two societies are sister organizations.

WIDER: Yes, they are. Emerson and Thoreau are two of the leading thinkers of the American Renaissance; naturally, study of them overlaps. In fact, many members of one organization belong to the other as well.

Since 2003, the Emerson Society has given considerable attention to its awards. We confer a graduate-student award for travel to conferences, an award that helps people publish, and the community or pedagogy award designed to help fund efforts so that Emerson's writings may reach beyond the classroom and into the community. I am most interested in encouraging this last award. The first person to whom we gave this award was a man working with a nature center in Texas and creating a trail guide using quotations from Emerson. The guides were available to anyone but were especially designed for schoolchildren on field trips.

While many people read Emerson, we want to stimulate more conversation about his work, both in the United States and in many different parts of the world. We are still working on that; perhaps it will take the form of an Internet chat room or something similar.

IKEDA: Your energetic, ambitious undertaking to go beyond the academic world and shed light on people attempting to spread Emerson's spirit in the real world is an important step in expanding the number of people who appreciate and understand his thought.

Though in a different arena, we present annual awards in the Soka Gakkai to people who have made contributions to their communities based on humanism. I proposed these awards in the spirit of my mentor, who urged us to value and recognize the contributions of people who work with dedication and devotion behind the scenes. My intent is to pick out, as with a searchlight, and honor these individuals who make untold and often unrecognized efforts.

In addition to these awards, I have written an essay series titled "Unforgettable Comrades," expressing my greatest respect and gratitude for the ordinary people, now deceased, who labored with us from the beginning of our movement—to record their efforts and achievements for posterity. I consider this my duty and mission as heir to my mentor and as the person guiding the development of the Soka Gakkai and the Soka Gakkai International.

WIDER: Would that more world leaders did the same. Your careful and considered attention to what each person contributes or has contributed provides a powerful model for social change.

Intellect without empathy is sterile. For too long, the dominant Western systems of thought have been those that distrust the role of empathic emotion.

Emerson, long identified as a man of the "head," whose philosophy excelled in and through pure abstraction, insisted in his essay on Montaigne that the "secrets of life are not shown except to sympathy and likeness."[8] When we study Emerson's writings about the mind's capabilities, we see how interested he was in all dimensions of thought, and how readily he included sympathy within his categories of mind. Though we may know him best for his ringing pronouncements on self-reliance, we would do well to remember that such reliance was based on a clear-eyed insight into the powerful relation between truth and tenderness (his terms).

In his essay "Friendship," he wrote:

> The end of friendship is a commerce the most strict and homely that can be joined; more strict than any of which we have experience. It is for aid and comfort through all the relations and passages of life and death.[9]

The "true relations" Emerson stressed have been central to the work you have so energetically devoted to members of the Soka Gakkai and the Soka Gakkai International.

IKEDA: You are far too generous in your praise. I am frequently asked by intellectuals from other countries or in interviews by the mass media how the SGI has grown to be a global organization. I always reply that it is because we value each individual to the highest degree. In everything I do, this is uppermost in my mind, and I have urged our leaders all over the world to adopt the same attitude. This is our only secret to success.

Throughout life, human beings encounter much pain and suffering—illness, the loss of loved ones, problems at work, at school, and with the children and family. The Soka Gakkai and the SGI have grown through lending an encouraging ear to people suffering the inevitable pains of birth, aging, sickness, and death by empathizing with their sufferings, encouraging them, and striving together to grace our lives with the joy of victory, assured of Nichiren's teaching that "when great evil occurs, great good follows."[10]

Each of us can make a sun rise from within our beings that cannot be vanquished by the harshest winter cold. We can make a garden of hope bloom from within our beings, announcing the spring of happiness, joy, and victory. This is our firm belief.

Nichiren teaches harmonious coexistence by employing the following metaphor: "If grasses wither, orchids grieve; if pine trees flourish, cypresses rejoice. Even trees and plants are so closely related."[11] In the words of a beloved song, "When you sorrow, I weep; when I rejoice, you dance."

The aim of our movement for human revolution is, by encouraging and supporting one another, to open the way for every individual to be happy.

CONVERSATION NINE

The Creative Life

IKEDA: To appreciate art is to encounter the realm of beauty and to experience the joy of creativity. It is also to discover the eternal and to awaken to the profundity of life.

The great twentieth-century American painter Georgia O'Keeffe loved the magnificent scenery of New Mexico, your home state. The works of her husband, Alfred Stieglitz, known by many as the father of modern photography, are also widely appreciated. The Tokyo Fuji Art Museum, which I founded, has in its collection several precious photographs he took of O'Keeffe.

I understand that you are fond of O'Keeffe's paintings and admire her way of life.

WIDER: I admire O'Keeffe's clarity of vision and purpose, whether in her life, in her words, in the blue of her New Mexico skies, or in the verticality of her New York buildings. She once commented that we rarely see what we are looking at. Her paintings confront us with the question: Do we see what is on the canvas or only the associations we bring to it? How do we open our eyes to what is daily in front of us?

Never deterred by what others thought of her or her work, she explored what most interested her. She recalled the resistance she received:

> I began talking about trying to paint New York. Of course, I was told that it was an impossible idea—even the men hadn't done too well with it. From my teens on I had been told that I had crazy notions so I was accustomed to disagreement and went on with my idea.[1]

IKEDA: Like her life, her style was distinctive and original. In addition to boldly dramatic, yet intricately detailed floral forms, she painted such things as roadside stones and animal bones. Her themes ranged from New York skyscrapers to desolate desert scenes. She painted whatever resonated with her aesthetic sensibilities, freely following her heart. Giving honest expression to her artistic creed, she once said to an art critic, "Why paint something if you don't love it?"[2]

When did she first visit New Mexico?

WIDER: It happened by accident, when she was thirty and traveling to Colorado with her younger sister. She had wanted to visit Colorado for a long time, and when this finally became possible during summer vacation, things didn't work out the way she had planned. Because a flood had washed out a railway bridge on the shortest route, they were rerouted by way of Albuquerque. Then, on her way back from Colorado, she stopped off at Santa Fe.

Laurie Lisle, one of O'Keeffe's biographers, describes the importance of this time: "Everything was drenched in the brilliant light of the high, dry desert air. 'I loved it immediately,' Georgia recalled later, 'From then on I was always on my way back.'"[3]

At the age of forty-one, she started living half of each year in

New Mexico and the other half in New York. After Alfred Stieglitz died, she moved to New Mexico permanently.

IKEDA: The O'Keeffe Art Museum in Santa Fe, the state capital of New Mexico, where she spent her late years, displays many of her works. Her series of paintings of single flowers that fill whole canvases are particularly famous in Japan. I have heard that this bold approach of magnifying the flowers to an extreme degree was motivated by her wish to force busy New Yorkers to stop and take a good look at flowers and really see them.

At one point, she said: "When you take a flower in your hand and really look at it . . . it's your world for the moment. I want to give that world to someone else."[4]

This approach corresponds with Emerson's artistic view: "What is a man but nature's finer success in self-explication? . . . What is his speech, his love of painting, love of nature, but a still finer success?"[5]

WIDER: I sense a correspondence between her style and your photographs and poetry. They invite us to take time and to see in a way that we may not have seen before. When we "look," do we "see truly," as Emerson might ask? Your photographs encourage us to see to the essence of things. They are dialogues as well. Even though we were not physically present at the time, we become part of the moment in which the picture was taken and are encouraged to respond vividly and directly.

IKEDA: You are kind to say so. Loving nature and discovering its wonder and beauty make one's life shine.

Nichiren Buddhism expounds the spirit of the Lotus Sutra, teaching that the "mind itself is the great earth, and that the great earth itself is the grasses and trees. . . . the moon itself is mind, and the flower itself is mind."[6] Buddhism teaches that looking with the "eye of the mind" and apprehending all the phenomena of the world from a profound view of life leads to a life of value and worth.

Great works of art, the distillation of the human soul, have the power to immeasurably elevate and enrich us. As Emerson wrote:

> Art should exhilarate, and throw down the walls of circumstance on every side, awakening in the beholder the same sense of universal relation and power which the work evinced in the artist, and its highest effect is to make new artists.[7]

WIDER: O'Keeffe's work powerfully demonstrates this "universal relation" of which Emerson spoke. Her work takes us to the essence of things and holds us there. Like your photographs, it is rooted in the spirit of penetrating beyond the casually seen outward appearances. In other words, she engages in dialogue with her subject matter, whether flowers, animal bones, or pebbles, and she expects the same of those who stand before her paintings.

GOOD TEACHERS

IKEDA: I can see why you appreciate her so much. Paintings are concrete realizations of the painter's sensibility and emotional and mental state. They are brilliant depictions of the artist's inner world. Buddhism expresses the wondrous function of life with the saying, "The mind is like a skilled painter."[8]

O'Keeffe was a woman always determined to live her own way, unwilling to compromise or submit to the expectations of others. This tendency was evident from her teens. Though she would have been looked on as a problem child at school, her school principal

Elizabeth Willis understood her and respected her independent nature. Willis had been head of a college art department and apparently valued O'Keeffe's talents and helped her in many ways.

WIDER: Such respect is essential. As young people explore and value their potential, they encounter powerful forces wielded by older generations. These generations can in turn empower, encouraging creativity and perceptiveness as did Willis for O'Keeffe. Unfortunately, this is often not the case, and instead of carefully listening to the insights of youth and to the questions they pose, the older generations thwart, rather than nurture, their independence and creativity.

IKEDA: To prevent this, adults must always be willing to learn from young people and develop together with them. They must have the depth and magnanimity to compassionately assist youth in reaching their full potential.

Willis continued to follow O'Keeffe's career after graduation and, when she began presenting her work publicly, commented in an alumnae journal on her making a name for herself as an artist in New York.[9] On several occasions, she traveled from Virginia to New York to attend O'Keeffe's exhibitions. The painter was moved to learn of this. Encountering good teachers is one of life's great joys.

WIDER: All my life, I have been blessed with caring, thought-provoking teachers. In high school, my English teacher Genevieve Charron inspired us with her eloquent respect for the literature she taught. I took several courses with her, and in each class, she helped us feel the importance of what we were studying. Whether it was Antigone's struggle against fixed authority or Job's questioning of undeserved misfortune, she taught us the profound power of poetic language to communicate the most pressing elements of life. She taught with a sense of wonder and discovery and responsibility, including all her students in this dynamic relationship.

I have always thought of reading as a great adventure. You never know where the next part of the story or the next idea may lead. There will be thoughts you have not before been able to form, images that will open your eyes and your heart. And there will also be moments of recognition, when you'll find yourself thinking, "Yes, this says exactly what I think or exactly what I feel, but I might never have thought to say it exactly in this way."

IKEDA: Genevieve Charron opened a new world of intellectual adventure to you, didn't she? One important role of teachers is to enable students to experience the source of wonder and the joy of discovery, and to develop the strength to advance on their own.

I had several unforgettable schoolteachers. Kohei Hiyama was my homeroom teacher in the fifth and sixth grades. One New Year, some of my classmates and I visited his house. Clad in traditional kimono, he welcomed us warmly. His wife had prepared sweet red-bean soup for us, and when we left, Mr. Hiyama saw us off at the door. He treated us schoolboys as adults. While he never tried to force his opinions on us, the sight of him was enough to put us on our good behavior. This was the kind of teacher he was.

The Chinese classic *Zizhi Tongjian* (Comprehensive Mirror for Aid in Government) said that though meeting a teacher of ordinary subjects is easy, meeting a teacher of life is hard. In this sense, I was fortunate indeed to encounter a teacher of such care and compassion in elementary school.

I fondly remember how, between classes, Mr. Hiyama used to read to us from historical novels like *Miyamoto Musashi*, widely considered to be one of Japan's greatest swordsmen, by the celebrated author Eiji Yoshikawa. His animated readings, accompanied by dramatic gestures, thrilled us all and transported us to the scene of action. His enjoyable classroom readings were also inspiration later on, when I became editor-in-chief of a boys' magazine at a publishing house run by my mentor.

In November 1973, more than thirty years after I graduated, Mr. Hiyama and his wife came to visit me. He had retired from his post as principal the preceding year. He expressed friendly concern about me and my busy schedule, which left me no time to rest, and urged me to take good care of myself.

At one class reunion, which I was unable to attend, he spoke of me to the others: "He doesn't need to be here. He's traveling the globe working for world peace."[10] Hearing of his remark, I was moved by his fond affection for former pupils who had graduated decades earlier. Mr. Hiyama passed away in 2004, but my gratitude to him lives in my heart.

To Never Retire

WIDER: It's moving to think how Mr. Hiyama stayed interested in his pupils all their lives. As a teacher, I want to demonstrate the same kind of affection for my students. Whether it is during their years at Colgate or long after their graduation, I want them to feel my ongoing interest in what challenges they face and what delights they enjoy.

I greatly esteem those students and teachers with the highest sense of vocation. They never retire.

IKEDA: Your comments remind me of another story. Once long ago, a certain king decided to confer an award on the most meritorious individual chosen from his people. The candidates, including many famous figures like rich men, physicians, scholars, and entrepreneurs, gathered at the palace. But selecting from among them proved difficult.

The final person to appear was an unknown, gray-haired woman who, though humble in appearance, glowed with the light of dignity, love, and wisdom. The king asked who she was.

One of his courtiers answered, "She is the one who has taught all of the other candidates."

Suddenly the chamber broke out in applause. The king descended from his throne to confer the honor of the highest rank on this mother of learning.

The outstanding educator forms human beings, creates the epoch, gives radiance to life, and makes peace shine forth. The merits of such a person will never fade. This story applies to you and the way you wholeheartedly encourage your students and desire their growth and development.

WIDER: Your comments fill me with great joy and strengthen my determination to continue on this path. Teaching has been a gift in my life. I want to celebrate all dedicated teachers. Even after he stopped working as a teacher and principal, Mr. Hiyama stayed on the educator's path.

In a similar way, Georgia O'Keeffe never retired but followed her chosen path as an artist to the end. As she got older and her eyesight deteriorated, she turned to pottery. It must have been hard to lose the ability to paint, to do what she once loved to do. But in pottery, she found another way to work with her own creativity. Here is another powerful role model, certainly for women, where youth has been so overemphasized, but probably for men as well.

IKEDA: Yes, it is. Buddhism teaches that people who live life deeply grow more youthful with increasing age. As Nichiren wrote, "You will grow younger, and your good fortune will accumulate."[11] The Buddhist teachings and faith exist for this purpose.

Life is a struggle. Art is a struggle. People who devote their whole beings to this struggle and triumph reveal their inner brilliance. In comparison, popularity and fame are only phantoms, extremely vulnerable to external influences and bringing no lasting happiness. As Buddhism teaches, even the joys felt in the realm of heaven are temporary and inevitably decay.

At one point, Georgia O'Keeffe said: "Success doesn't come with painting one picture. It is building step by step against great odds."[12] These are words of truth. On another occasion, when feeling downcast, she realized, the "thing I enjoy of the autumn is there no matter what is happening to me."[13] Then she painted "Yellow Hickory Leaves with Daisy." Her optimistic, vigorous way of life continues to encourage many people.

WIDER: Several programs at the Georgia O'Keeffe Museum speak directly to this. For example, there is the Art and Leadership Program for Women, in which creative expression and leadership are not separated. For middle schoolers, workshops draw on the students' "creative interests . . . to foster the development of leadership skills, build confidence, and encourage the setting of ambitious goals." The program began as a program for girls and has recently been expanded to include a program for boys as well.

IKEDA: I hope that many young people will learn from O'Keeffe's example how to overcome life's hardships cheerfully and lead strong, creative lives.

Nearly forty years ago, while writing a collection of essays that a Japanese firm published as *Watashi no jinsei-kan* (My View of Life), I fell ill from exhaustion. My temperature went up to 100 or 102 degrees Fahrenheit. Nevertheless, I continued writing, page after page, keeping track of the number of pages on a separate sheet until the manuscript was complete. Later I gave that scorecard of completed pages to my eldest son as a memento.

In one of the essays, I commented:

I hope that women who raise children and know in their flesh and bones the precious nature of life will become active in still stronger leadership roles in today's society, with its prevailing tendency to devalue life.

We need to cultivate greater respect for the lives of wise, strong women and humbly learn from them.

WIDER: Many of your written works are crystallizations of suffering and effort, like the one you describe. I am also deeply impressed by the support you derive from the presence of your wife, Mrs. Kaneko Ikeda. When I first met the two of you in 2006, I was struck by her radiant energy and vibrant smile. In a comparable way to O'Keeffe's paintings and your photographs, her life leads us from appearance to essence. Here is the strength of your lives together—a half-century of deeply understood companionship.

I feel that her strength and beauty are generated by her belief in the deep bonds that can form between human hearts. Such bonds have nothing to do with superiority or inferiority but result from togetherness founded on mutual trust. They impart great strength.

CONVERSATION TEN

Renaissance Women

IKEDA: Time is constantly passing, and society is always changing, but the great spirits transcend time and national boundaries,
elevating people's hearts and illuminating the future. This is why
I like to give young people as many opportunities as I can to learn
from the noble spirits and ideas of the great. This is also the reason that on the campuses of Soka University of Japan and Soka
Women's College, we have statues of outstanding individuals who
dedicated themselves to peace, humanity, and culture, such as Victor Hugo, Leo Tolstoy, Walt Whitman, Leonardo da Vinci, Marie
Curie, and Alisher Navoi.

In September 2009, we added at Soka University of Japan a
statue of the Indian poet Rabindranath Tagore, presented by the
Indian Council for Cultural Relations. On the pedestal of the
statue, a Tagore quotation is engraved: "It is the mission of civilization to bring unity among people and establish peace and harmony."[1] Located in a plaza between the Center for International
Exchanges, where students from many countries study, and the
Graduate School of Education, the statue watches over the development of world citizens who bear the responsibility for the

new century. Students gazing up to the statue derive profound intellectual, spiritual, and poetic inspiration from the daily sight of Tagore's majestic figure.

WIDER: *Where* we learn profoundly affects *how* and *what* we learn. As human beings, we have tremendous imaginative capacity—but we need prompts for our imagination. At Soka University, students and faculty daily see inspiring lives embodied in the very places where they live, work, and study. Every time they walk by one of these statues, the artists' powerful renditions reach out, asking those who pass to pause, take the imaginative leap, and dedicate their own lives to realizing peace with justice and beauty.

Tagore was of special interest to my Emerson professors Paul Schmidt and Gail Baker. I have powerful memories of Paul reading Tagore's poetry aloud.

IKEDA: Reading aloud is important. And reading poetry aloud has the power to awaken the inner spirit and open people's hearts. Indeed, much of the poetry of ancient times was created specifically to be recited. I am delighted to learn that your mentors introduced you to Tagore's poetry, which I have loved from my youth.

Born in 1861, this great poet who connected East and West stressed the need to move beyond our civilization of power, characterized by violence and conflict, toward a new civilization of harmony. He also expressed high hopes for the role women would play in this transformation. Tagore held that men regard their fellows mostly in terms of power and ability; a man's interest in his fellow beings becomes real when he finds in them some special gift of power or usefulness, whereas women see others differently.

Tagore wrote:

> A woman feels interest in her fellow-beings because they
> are living creatures, because they are human, not because
> of some particular purpose which they can serve, or some

power which they possess and for which she a special admiration.[2]

In other words, the major source of women's interest is their affection for and sensitivity to human beings and life. This attitude seems to resonate with Emerson's views on women.

WIDER: While Emerson drew wisely upon the methods of inquiry in which men had been trained, he was also keenly aware of their limitations. He valued intuition, which he called a higher sort of seeing, as more direct and more quickly perceptive than the critical approach he saw men generally using. Although he could be distrustful of emotion—a faculty of human perception he associated with women—he nonetheless saw how women's insight was more comprehensive than men's, and how women more readily perceived and understood the correspondences, the interconnections, on which the universe was built.

Emerson enthusiastically cultivated associations with women who demonstrated this power of perception, and he wanted to pioneer a new age in which women's voices could be heard. He encouraged and supported them in mutually inspiring ways. One such woman was Emma Lazarus, the poet we know for lines engraved on the base of the Statue of Liberty. He was supportive of her poetry when many, due to their own prejudices, were not. Emma Lazarus was Jewish when anti-Semitism was the rule in the United States, a rule Emerson gladly broke.

IKEDA: France presented the Statue of Liberty to the United States as a sign of friendship in 1876, on the occasion of the centennial of Independence Day. The sculptor Frédéric August Bartholdi is said to have modeled the face on that of his mother, who lost her husband early in life and raised her children alone. For Bartholdi, no doubt, no image shone as magnificently as his mother's visage.

The statue's pose, raising the torch of freedom high in her right hand and clasping a tablet with the Declaration of Independence in her left, is said to be based on that of a young girl Bartholdi saw when he was a young man: In 1851, there was a popular uprising against Napoleon III (Louis-Napoléon). As a crowd of people stood before a barricade, a young woman holding a burning torch aloft stepped forth to lead a charge across the barricades. At this instant, a shot rang out, and the girl fell, but the fire from her torch spread, and the barricades crumbled. This anonymous though noble woman became one of the models for the Statue of Liberty.

Similar statues were erected in many places in France. I fondly remember seeing one on the banks of the Seine in Paris. Bartholdi's drawings of the statue are among the Soka University treasures.

WIDER: It was during the time of Louis-Napoléon that Emerson's good friend Margaret Fuller traveled to Europe as the first American female foreign correspondent assigned there. In addition to writing her well-known book *Woman in the Nineteenth Century*, she was a correspondent for the *New York Tribune* and wrote on some of the toughest issues of the day: abuse of people committed to insane asylums; prisons and abuse of prisoners; and slavery and the need for the United States to abolish it. She was in Europe during the 1848 revolutions and took an active part in Italy.

Through her writing, she was a voice of conscience insisting that readers were complicit if they did nothing. Were she alive today, I think it would be hard for her to choose a single profession. In some ways, she was a sociologist; in some ways, a philosopher; and in other ways, a historian. Above all, she was certainly a civil-rights activist.

IKEDA: Fuller was so intellectually accomplished that she was permitted to use the Harvard library at a time when women were not admitted to universities. She became famous as a person of passion and determination who fought to tear down many of the daunting social barriers of her time.

In her youth, she struggled. Losing her father when she was twenty-five, she worked as a language teacher to help with family expenses. Her meeting with Emerson in Boston was a major turning point in her life.

What impression do you believe this first encounter with Fuller made on Emerson?

SELF-RELIANCE IN WOMEN

WIDER: When he met someone like Margaret Fuller, Emerson must have thought: "Aha! This is how self-reliance works in women." I think that he wished there were more women like her. Though she was seven years his junior, he found his relationship with Margaret Fuller similar to the one he had with Mary Moody Emerson, although, of course, in different terms because of their differences in age and philosophical grounding.

Emerson valued intellect and felt that, through its power, humans could powerfully analyze the world. Fuller challenged his understanding of intellect, questioning whether the mind functioned well if it narrowly used only certain of its capabilities. She championed all faculties of the mind. If she felt he was dealing with a subject inadequately or incompletely, she would ask him to pause and approach the issue with a different way of thinking.

He might have demurred with the excuse that it wasn't what his mind could do. She felt that minds were more elastic, more flexible, able to think in many different ways. I think this was both a great challenge and a great lesson.

IKEDA: You bring their dialogues vividly to life for me. Fuller was editor-in-chief of Emerson's literary journal *The Dial* (published from 1840 to 1844), which not only presented to society at large the ideas of Emerson and the Transcendentalists but also introduced other cutting-edge thought of the time. It introduced Eastern philosophy and was the first publication in the United States to carry an English-language translation of part of the Lotus Sutra, the chapter titled "The Parable of the Medicinal Herbs."

WIDER: Emerson originated and championed the idea of including key selections from the great wisdom traditions of the world. The "Medicinal Herbs" section was particularly thought provoking for the Transcendentalists.

IKEDA: "The Parable of the Medicinal Herbs" proclaims the equality of all life and the relationship of harmonious coexistence among all things. It also illuminates the Buddha's life condition, a state in which wisdom equals compassion, and compassion equals wisdom. At the same time, it presents a world in which each human being can bring to fragrant bloom the flower of his or her rich individuality.

Going back to Margaret Fuller, she made friends in Europe with a fellow female writer, the French novelist George Sand. One of Sand's letters contains a compelling passage to the effect that, though at great personal peril and risk she had poured everything she had into her many novels, no publisher had been able to promote—or even tried to promote—them. She went on to say that, without overestimating the value of her own writings, she would do whatever she could to bring works that did everything possible to instruct and elevate people of all classes to all those interested in reading them. Despite numerous obstacles, Sand did her utmost for the sake of humanity and society through her writing and publishing.

Fuller added the power of education to the power of the written word as a weapon in her social activism. To this end, she abandoned the financial stability of a teaching career to begin conversation classes for women who, like herself, could not attend universities.

WIDER: Her conversation classes were epoch-making. Her idea was to create situations in which women could continue their education. At the time, young women were fortunate if they could participate in some kind of high school education at women's academies. Even then, etiquette and women's so-called accomplishments (for example, fancy needlework and dancing) were often given more attention than developing the young mind's ability to pursue thought or "free and frank inquiry" as it was called in those days.

Typically Fuller held her conversations on the same days that Emerson lectured, so that women could attend both as part of an educational package. She also had women write papers, so that they formulated their ideas systematically.

The topics were fascinating and important. She focused on mythology, especially Greek mythology, because she felt that such stories held powerful keys to human behavior. She also broached big topics that even today we often shy away from. How rarely do we consider questions such as "what is life" or "what is inspiration"? If her students gave her answers that she felt were too vague, she would, like a Socrates, question them in order to prompt them into going further.

The power and importance of her conversation classes cannot be overestimated. They shaped a generation of women in remarkable ways. Talking about the effect of these conversations, one woman said, "Perhaps I could best express it by saying that I was no longer the limitation of myself but I felt the whole wealth of the universe was open to me."

IKEDA: The spiritual foundation of the American Renaissance consisted of two major elements. One was the literary culture of books and journals. The other was the lecture culture, of which Emerson and Thoreau were enthusiastic proponents. In each community, lectures were open to everyone, both sexes and all ages.

Margaret Fuller took full advantage of the opportunities offered by the public lecture, devoting unsparing passion and enthusiasm to enabling women, subject to onerous social restrictions, to obtain through this venue the education they needed in order to realize their full potential as human beings.

As I already explained (see Conversation Five), Tsunesaburo Makiguchi did something similar a century ago by initiating correspondence courses for women. Having had the experience of teaching geography in private girls' schools, Makiguchi, like Margaret Fuller, wanted to provide educational opportunities for young women who, for one reason or another, found further schooling impossible. With this aim, he published correspondence-course materials and journals, and energetically took it upon himself to lecture in many parts of the country.

In the spirit of his undertaking, I founded in 1973 the Soka Girls' Junior and Senior High Schools (now coeducational, as the Kansai Soka Junior and Senior High Schools) in Katano, Osaka. As I mentioned before (see Conversation One), on the occasion of the first entrance ceremony, I made the following remarks to the incoming students:

> It is my hope that all of you will achieve the realization that your own happiness can never be built on the misfortune of others. The world is vast, and these Soka schools may seem like tiny poppy seeds in comparison. But the fundamental point is that your seemingly small daily efforts themselves will contribute to the path of peace for all humanity and eventually give rise to a force that will encompass the world. I firmly believe this.

I visited the schools repeatedly, motivated by my desire to build a tradition of exemplary education for girls as envisioned by Mr. Makiguchi. I've played tennis and ping-pong with the students and visited classrooms, speaking with individual students and encouraging them. The experience gained at the Soka Girls' Junior and Senior High Schools reached fruition in the creation of Soka Women's College. In 1982, the junior and senior highs became coeducational.

PHILOSOPHY OF THE PEOPLE

WIDER: Understanding that we cannot build our own happiness on the misfortune of others is a great guideline for human life. I am deeply touched by your hands-on approach to the creation and growth of your schools. And I know from experience how vibrant are the educational opportunities for girls and women in the Soka schools. Every time I have visited, I have been so heartened by the students' dedication both to learning and to being peacemakers in whatever they do. As you know, I have a special place in my heart for Soka Women's College.

In *Woman in the Nineteenth Century*, Margaret Fuller wanted to give women a sense of their own history. She devoted many pages to the long line of women—across all time and around the world—who were strong leaders in their own right. She discusses those in positions of government power (for example, Elizabeth I) as well as those who pioneered new ideas and practices for their societies (for example, abolitionist Angelina Grimké).

Her conversation classes tried to build ways for women to imagine themselves and to see themselves differently from the way society painted them. The classes powerfully affected not only the women who attended at the time but also their children and the coming generations.

Fuller's classes were preceded by the so-called reading parties and historical conferences organized by Elizabeth Palmer Peabody, who also wanted to give women an opportunity to gather for intellectual conversation. In conventional social situations, this just didn't happen. So she organized her discussions around a set of readings that allowed the women to explore new subjects and hone their intellectual abilities.

IKEDA: Both can be called pioneering undertakings. Scenes of dialogue like this represent democracy in a microcosm.

In addition to her interest in lifelong education, Elizabeth Palmer Peabody is famous for having pioneered juvenile education by creating, in Boston, the first English-language kindergarten in the United States. Her achievements served as a useful reference when I, too, founded kindergartens.

It is said that many Transcendentalists, including Emerson and Thoreau, visited Peabody's bookstore to take advantage of its extensive range of works on oriental thought.

WIDER: She was a learned woman. We should also remember that the bookstore and Foreign Circulating Library she ran made books available in the Boston community for those not affiliated with Harvard, including translations of the different wisdom traditions from Buddhism, Hinduism, and Confucianism. She provided space in the store for Margaret Fuller to hold her conversations. The store became a magnet for people as a place to gather and exchange ideas. She provided books and an ever-ready space to make certain that intellectual exchange could in fact take place.

IKEDA: You attended the forum on "Re-awakening East-West Connections: Walden and Beyond" at the Ikeda Center for Peace, Learning, and Dialogue in Cambridge, Massachusetts, in 2004. On that occasion, Professor Alan Hodder of Hampshire College spoke of Emerson's passion for studying Indian philosophy and religion, in which he found thoughts that harmonized with his own.

Professor Hodder added that the influence of Indian philosophy and religion was even more powerful on Thoreau, who learned attitudes concerning the pursuit of spiritual experience.

On the same occasion, Phyllis Cole, then president of the Ralph Waldo Emerson Society, stressed the importance of women as supporters of Emerson's and Thoreau's activities. For example, Margaret Fuller held mixed gender conversation classes—a rather radical idea at the time—to discuss Emerson's ideas. At one such class, according to Dr. Cole, a young woman proposed the idea that "if women would learn a new mental concentration, future poetry might emanate from her home and exert a power to bless and heal the nations so that 'Men shall learn war no more.'"[3]

My discussion with you has reaffirmed my impression of the fundamental role of women like Peabody and Fuller in the American Renaissance.

WIDER: Theirs was an age of incredible women. I've often wished I could go back to that period and be part of the conversations. The issues that they were thinking about, and the way they were thinking about them, are tremendously exciting, because they were trying to find a philosophy that would come directly into lived experience. It is not a philosophy isolated from the people. It is, as Emerson said, a philosophy of the people.

I would especially like to have met Caroline Sturgis, one of Fuller's disciples. She had a brilliant mind and was an independent thinker. Emerson describes her as a new sun. Her thinking was so independent and her willingness to challenge social conventions so direct that her actions and comments burst forth like a new sun arising.

She was a voracious reader, as all these women were. Always interested in ideas that were new to her, she clearly benefited from the wealth of books in Elizabeth Peabody's Foreign Circulating Library. She certainly would have read the selection from the

Lotus Sutra in *The Dial*, and her poetry also shows influences of the *Bhagavad Gita*.

IKEDA: The Lotus Sutra clearly proclaims that women can attain Buddhahood. This teaching represents a philosophy of life that liberates the immeasurable power of women, enabling them to make a new sun rise from their innermost beings and opening a path of profound mission for them.

India, where the Lotus Sutra originated, was a source of fascination for flag bearers of the American Renaissance, such as Emerson, Thoreau, and Whitman. Today in India, one institution dealing with the challenge of female education is the Soka Ikeda College of Arts and Science for Women, founded in Chennai in August 2000 by my friend the poet and educator Sethu Kumanan. In a letter he sent to me on the opening of the college, he said that the origin of his college was the achievements of Soka education for women, whom he called a "world superpower." At his strong urging as chairman of the college, I agreed to be its honorary founder, and my wife accepted the position of honorary principal.

Dr. Kumanan became interested in Soka education after Krishna Srinivas, president of the World Poetry Society Intercontinental, introduced my poem "Mother" to him.

WIDER: I understand how Dr. Kumanan feels about your poem. I was deeply moved by a musical rendition of "Mother" by a string ensemble at the Soka schools, where I was visiting and talking with students. And I vividly remember the inspiring vibrancy of the White Lily Chorus beautifully singing "Mother" at the Soka International Women's Center.

IKEDA: I published the poem in praise of all the great mothers of the world, though my own mother provided the immediate inspiration. When she became ill and I was too busy to go home, thinking of her constantly, I composed verses that, when further developed, became the finished poem. Not long after it was set to music and presented publically, my mother died. I never had a chance to read it to her in person. I had a tape recording of it sent to her, however, and I am told that she smiled when it was played at her bedside.

Later, students of the Soka Junior and Senior High Schools performed it for Dr. Kumanan, who said that it reminded him of his own mother, laboring hard milking cattle in a poor country village to make money for her son's schooling. Because of this experience, he made up his mind to open a college in a rural area. He said that when young women from harsh situations have the opportunity to study happily at his school and go on to become beacons of hope for their families and communities, India will have opened the way to a new century of women. He wishes, he added, to take the first step in this direction. His words delighted me because they mean that the spirit of Tsunesaburo Makiguchi is blooming in another part of the world.

At present, as part of Madras University, the college is achieving great things. It has been cited for excellence in female education by the nationwide advisory committee of the Indian Council of Gandhian Studies and is highly regarded by former president A. P. J. Abdul Kalam and leaders from many areas of Indian society.

WIDER: I was privileged to meet Dr. Kumanan at the Toda Institute conference in November 2009 and celebrate his marvelous work. I hope someday to visit the school. The education of girls and women is the key to building cultures of peace.

Another significant emphasis in Margaret Fuller's *Woman in the Nineteenth Century* is the importance of opportunity. Without opportunity, potential withers. How can individuals know what they can do unless they are given the chance to find out? Once they discover this ability, whatever it happens to be, they need the opportunity to learn how to cultivate it and, of course, to practice what they learn.

To this day, women lack such opportunities. This is the great challenge being addressed by both the Soka Ikeda College of Arts and Science for Women in India and Soka Women's College.

IKEDA: Your comments will certainly please Dr. Kumanan. He often joins with the students in dialogue and has said that all of them come from poor families with problems. Some of them have lost all respect for their parents but become caring daughters once poetry has helped them overcome their anguish. Dr. Kumanan insists that, as the students of the Soka Ikeda College of Arts and Science for Women know better than anyone else, the first step to peace takes place within the family.

Unfortunately, many women in the world still lack opportunities for adequate education. Twenty-first-century society will not improve or fully develop until this situation is remedied. The world today stands in growing need of women like Fuller, Peabody, and Sturgis, who, together with Emerson and Thoreau, invigorated a broad segment of society with the breadth of the American Renaissance. I am absolutely convinced that this will be the light source illuminating a new renaissance of life.

Strength Through Connection

IKEDA: Nichiren employs the metaphor of a "lantern lighting up a place that has been dark for a hundred, a thousand, or ten thousand years."[1] The principled actions of women who, in times shrouded by the darkness of the harshest adversity, have illuminated others with their lives and led their eras toward hope, peace, and happiness, are like the lantern described by Nichiren.

The noble members of our Soka Gakkai and SGI women's and young women's divisions are striving for their own happiness and the happiness of others by empathizing with and encouraging countless people in difficulties. The Soka International Women's Center, which opened in Shinanomachi, Tokyo, in September 2000, on the eve of the new century, is a palace of peace and happiness in honor of these women and mothers. In September 2010, it celebrated its tenth anniversary. Since its opening, many guests from overseas have visited the building and formed expanding, overlapping networks of dialogue and beautiful friendship. We are grateful to you for having visited the center in the autumn of 2009.

WIDER: It is I who am grateful. I greatly admire the women of the SGI and was honored to visit the beautiful Soka International Women's Center. It was a most wonderful occasion, especially since the day of my visit was November 18, Soka Gakkai Founding Day. I was met with warmth and enthusiasm. Everyone immediately made me feel at home, and as we toured the rooms, Mrs. Kasanuki, who was at that time director of the Women's Peace and Culture Department, and Mrs. Tsukiji, who was then chairperson for the Women's Peace Committee, kindly assured me that there is a true home for me there any time I can return. And for Taiward, too!

IKEDA: By all means, you and your child—and your husband, too—are welcome to visit as often as you like. Everyone was delighted to engage in significant discussions with you. Members of both the women's and young women's divisions are eagerly looking forward to welcoming you again as an ambassador of peace and the poetic spirit.

WIDER: The women's center embodies the strength created when women work together for peace with justice. As you say, it is indeed a "palace of peace and happiness." When I was there, I strongly felt the goodwill and good cheer of all the women who have worked within its rooms. What they do has a lasting effect that extends far beyond the center itself. It is a center in the best sense of the word—a strong place within which individuals gather and renew their strength as they head outward to build peace cultures throughout the world. The building itself is beautiful, and I deeply appreciate how its beauty so powerfully communicates your own encouragement of women's work for peace.

I found your photograph of a single road stretching through the green fields at Windsor Castle particularly evocative. We all can find ourselves traveling on such a road, no matter where it is physically located for us. I was moved to learn that the center's most prominent chandelier—modeled after a sailing ship, the center's symbol—represents the Soka women's approach to life: converting all winds into tail winds ensuring harmonious, forward motion and progress. Hearing this reminded me of Emerson's words written for the women whose thoughts and actions he admired: "O friend, never strike sail to a fear! Come into port greatly."[2]

IKEDA: A powerful message. As Emerson declared, in our journey through life, we must never strike the sails that carry us forward. Sailing ships were often referred to as "ladies of the sea" because of their awe-inspiring beauty and steadfast courage in cleaving the billows and pressing onward to their destinations.

Like Emerson, the nineteenth-century Russian poet Nikolay Yazykov wrote of sailing ships advancing in the storm:

> On the sea the cloud falls sudden,
> Wind blows fierce, black billows form,
> Tempest threatens: on we struggle,
> Match our courage with the storm....
> Courage, friend! though storms be raging,
> On, with steadfast course, I sail.[3]

I understand that when the Chinese historian Zhang Kaiyuan and his wife, Huang Huaiyu, visited the Soka International Women's Center, she said of the chandelier:

> Women don't improve themselves by relying on men and the people around them. They must acquire their rights independently and move forward, riding the waves and bucking the current. This sailing ship calls on all women to do that.

She and her husband added these words of praise: "Soka Gakkai women are our role models!"

WIDER: I want to underscore the importance of Huang Huaiyu's words. Too often women have been taught both in school and at home to follow rather than to lead, to wait to respond rather than to initiate needed thought and action. As Margaret Fuller urged more than 150 years ago:

> We would have every arbitrary barrier thrown down. We would have every path laid open to Woman as freely as to Man. . . . though I might be aided and instructed by others, I must depend on myself as the only constant friend. This self-dependence, which was honored in me, is deprecated as a fault in most women. They are taught to learn their rule from without, not to unfold it from within.[4]

I greatly appreciate the words of encouragement you pen for others, so that every person may grow each in her or his own way. I was again strongly reminded of this at the women's center. Seeing your writing desk, which now makes its home there, also gave me pause to think about your own daily practice of writing, about what was written at that very desk, as well as what you are writing now.

When I had the great joy of meeting you and Mrs. Ikeda in 2006, I immediately felt your vibrant, energetic commitment to promoting peace through the harmonious development of human potential. Both of you radiate happiness and convey the great and wonderful prospects that lie before us. Meeting with you was one of these life-centering experiences for me. Especially in American university systems, it is easy to feel isolated when social justice is the heart of your work. Meeting you reminded me again how large the true world of humanity is and where our true homes are found.

IKEDA: For my wife and me, meeting you has been a treasured part of our lives. It has been an encounter with the vibrancy of American poetry, with the soul of a courageous, engaged educator, and with the spirit of caring for life embodied by the sterling characters of both you and your mother.

My wife feels that she is a constant participant in the discussions between you and me.

WIDER: I am always attracted by the words your wife, Kaneko, chooses to share in a given place. I especially remember these words shared by your wife with her characteristic forthrightness: "Complaints erase good fortune. Grateful prayer builds happiness for all eternity." These words articulate the power an individual can bring to the most difficult circumstances. Hearing these words, I thought how strongly my mother would agree. These sentiments were close to her heart.

I often thought about my mother during my visit to the women's center. She would have loved meeting the women there and would have appreciated the calm, purposeful, and vibrant feel in the rooms themselves. She was always sensitive to place and knew that, if you listened with your whole being, a place would teach you many things.

A LARGER MUSIC

IKEDA: Mothers are vast and deep as a great sea. In "Mother," I wrote of a mother's love:

> *Deeper than the sea.*
> *The profundity of your love seems*
> *Beyond grasp.*

The modern Japanese poet Tatsuji Miyoshi noted that the French word for mother, *la mère*, resembles the word for sea, *la mer*, and that the Chinese character meaning "sea" contains an element meaning "mother."

The rich poetic spirit shared by you and your wise mother seems to reverberate with the wondrous workings of life, like the music of the surf caressing the shore.

WIDER: The sea gives us a beautiful, evocative image of strength through connection. At the women's center, I thought about Mom when I saw the French doll Mrs. Ikeda played with as a child. My mother loved dolls and was always eager to find out their stories: where they came from and what had happened to them in the past. She collected and studied them, because she felt that to understand a country's culture and history, you needed to know about the children's lives—especially about their toys and the stories they told.

She believed in studying history through the world of children. Hers was—and is—a very unusual idea. Paying attention to children's lives is one pivotal way to build cultures of peace.

IKEDA: Your mother was wonderfully perceptive. In the same spirit as your mother, starting in 1990, we of the Soka Gakkai began sponsoring the exhibitions "The World's Toys and Education" and "Toys Around the World" throughout Japan. We feature about a thousand toys from a hundred countries and regions. Each of them epitomize mothers' affection, sincerity, and ingenuity. To date, more than two million people have attended the exhibitions.

The hearts of children the world over are pure and innocent, no matter what country they're from. Finding ways to inspire and motivate these emissaries from the future should be one of our main focuses if we wish to enable humanity to advance together single-mindedly toward peace.

WIDER: At the women's center, I was interested to see a model of the house you and Mrs. Ikeda lived in when you were first married. It had a piano, which, I understand, you learned to play. Since I, too, play piano and have seen the great joy music can bring, I was delighted and deeply touched to learn from one of the women that you often played the piano to encourage and bring joy into the minds of your valued comrades.

IKEDA: My wife, who plays the piano fairly well, taught me. I decided to learn when I heard her play the song "Dainanko" (The Great Lord Kusunoki), a song about the bond of trust and love between parent and child, which my mentor loved. I hoped to play for the pleasure of our comrades.

Since my youth, I have loved music. Times were very hard in Japan after World War II. Even so, I scraped together what little money I could to buy a phonograph, occasionally borrowed records from friends, and listened to the masterpieces of classical music. I fondly recall inviting fellow youth division members to my house to discuss our dreams for the future as we listened to Beethoven's Fifth Symphony or von Suppé's Light Cavalry Overture.

You mentioned that your mother learned about the culture and history of other countries through dolls; I think music can provide the same service. Of course, music is a language common all over the world. It is the rhythm of culture, communicating the vibrancy of the human spirit. It also possesses the power of peace, uniting individuals and peoples.

Music plays an important part in the Soka Gakkai and the SGI, and as we promote our movement, we value it highly. Our culture centers all over Japan have pianos. We also have bands, fife-and-drum corps, and choral groups throughout Japan and the world. Their performances are a great source of inspiration and encouragement. They participate in local parades and other events.

WIDER: I have long wished that more attention would be given both to making music and to listening fully to music. There is no greater power, especially making music with others. If the leaders in our institutions—governmental, educational, and even military—could act more like musicians, gathering to hear and learn from one another's music, and collaborate on new ways of creating a larger music, then cultures of peace would arise where violence now rules. Here the ordinary citizens lead their leaders.

I have seen this amply demonstrated time and again by SGI members—whether hearing the string quartet that played for me at Soka High School, singing the school song with students at Soka Women's College, or delighting in the White Lily Chorus at the Soka International Women's Center. Their powerful voices expressed the strength of women working together for a world of greater understanding.

A TIME TO LISTEN

IKEDA: As I said before, I conducted a dialogue with the genius violinist Sir Yehudi Menuhin (see Conversation Six). On that occasion, he told me: "Human beings can directly contact and harmonize themselves with the vibrations of the universe. Music is one way in which this is expressed, as is art."[5]

We agreed that, for the sake of peace, human beings need to learn self-discipline and to control their minds. Preserving the balance that is characteristic of fine music, we need to transform, elevate, and expand ourselves.

Human life has many dimensions—joy and sorrow, compassion and anger, pleasure and sadness. Each of these life conditions resonates with the vibrations of the universe. This is explained in the Buddhist principle of "three thousand realms in a single moment of life"—the idea that "three thousand realms," or all phenomena, exist within each moment of an individual's life, and that every such moment has infinite potential. This principle also teaches that all people possess the Buddha nature—the supreme state of life—and can manifest it in their daily behavior.

This Buddhist philosophy presents a way to vibrantly adorn our lives, as we powerfully sound the melody of joy and mission unique to each of us—the way to act for the sake of society, undaunted by the winds of adversity, while cultivating our lives and working in harmony with others to make the world a better place.

The Buddhist scriptures also emphasize that the power of listening is as important as the power of the voice. You stressed this in your keynote address at the international conference sponsored by the Toda Institute for Global Peace and Policy Research at Soka University in November 2009.

WIDER: Listening is a pivotal yet often overlooked value. At my parents' home, a plaque hung in an often-seen place reminded the reader to "Take time." In her own handwriting, Mom added, "Take time to listen."

As I observe those of us in the United States today, I see and hear how we live in an almost relentlessly noisy age. Televisions drone in the background; people talk to those they are with while texting someone else. Mechanical noises surround us.

It is difficult to find places of true quiet. Difficult, but necessary. This quiet is always within us—in the pulse of our heartbeat, in the space of our breath—and when we ourselves begin to listen to our inner stillness, we can begin to listen, truly listen, to others. Such listening, with interest and without judgment, is key for building cultures of peace.

IKEDA: Buddhism explains the ineffable dignity of human life on many levels. For example, Nichiren wrote:

> It [your body] is the treasure tower adorned with the seven kinds of treasures—hearing the correct teaching, believing it, keeping the precepts, engaging in meditation, practicing assiduously, renouncing one's attachments, and reflecting on oneself.[6]

In other words, the spiritual treasures of willingness to hear, powerful faith, self-control and self-discipline, unshakeable resolution, unrelenting progress, refusal to obsess over distress or hardship, and humble self-examination are what adorn human life. The desire to hear the correct teaching heads the list. Creating a world of peace founded on respect for the dignity of life begins with listening to the voice of truth and sincerely heeding it for the sake of justice.

WIDER: Willingness to listen is essential to justice. No wonder it is one of the precious elements in the treasure tower. I appreciate your instruction in this profound aspect of Buddhist philosophy.

Women's division members in Japan taught me that the kanji used to write the word *kiku*—hear—is made up of an element standing for the ear and other elements signifying fourteen minds. By the word itself, we are challenged to listen attentively and expansively, so that we might hear and value multiple perspectives, multiple minds, without confusing this manifold richness with cacophony.

Too often, where words could celebrate and realize the richness of possibility in human communities, they become barriers and even weapons. When we fail to learn who the person we are conversing with truly is, we run the risk of creating divisions or of silencing another.

In contrast, your words build bridges of encouragement, so that others might cross into the realm of open exchange where all freely share their creativity, their way of living poetry in this world. Here is the spirit of dialogue embodied and indeed the spirit of democracy.

IKEDA: You've been mentioning "cultures of peace." August 2010 was the sixty-fifth anniversary of World War II's end. It was an unbelievably cruel, horrendous war, in which many precious lives were lost.

Yet conflict and internal strife continue around the world, and humanity remains unable to break the chains of violence and hatred that hold it captive. These circumstances have given rise to numerous popular grassroots movements calling for peace.

Within the Soka Gakkai, the Women's Peace Committee and other groups have taken up the challenge of steadily working to plant in society the culture of peace. One aspect of this has been the exhibition "Women and the Culture of Peace," seen by 970,000 people in twenty-nine cities throughout Japan. Another exhibition, "Children and the Culture of Peace," has been seen by 880,000 people in 128 cities. In addition, 200,000 people have participated in our peace-culture forums held in more than 300 locales. All of these activities have stimulated tremendous reactions.

These activities of women for peace were inspired by the publication of *Heiwa e no negai o komete* (In the Hope of Peace), compiled by women's division members from the testimonies of about 500 World War II survivors. The compilation took ten years and resulted in a twenty-volume series that has been praised as a grassroots history of the war in the words of ordinary citizens and a precious legacy of humanity's aspirations for peace.

In April 2009, the SGI released a DVD, *Testimonies of Hiroshima and Nagasaki: Women Speak Out for Peace*, which contains excerpts of this series in English, Spanish, French, Chinese, and Japanese that explain the immorality of nuclear weapons and call for their abolition. It, too, has provoked deeply felt reactions.

In May 2010, in connection with the NPT (Treaty on the Non-Proliferation of Nuclear Weapons) Review Conference, SGI youth representatives presented to the United Nations a petition signed by 2,270,000 people calling for the abolition of nuclear weapons. In an interview with the Inter Press Service, I was asked my opinion on the conference results, and I replied that to broaden the movement for a nuclear-free world, it is essential to further unite the voices of ordinary people seeking peace.

WIDER: At the Soka International Women's Center, I engaged in meaningful conversations about peace-building initiatives and peace education projects with members of the Women's Peace Committee and the Young Women's Conference for Peace and Culture. I learned about their campaign to publish women's wartime experiences, which you just mentioned. Their work is monumental.

All too often, the daily experiences of those living in war zones have gone unrecorded. Attention is paid to the military but not to those who live daily in the midst of violence. Without direct knowledge of war's actual brutalities, it is all too easy for a glorified version of violence to become dominant.

I see this dominance now in the United States, where so many people think first about literally and violently "fighting" for "our" freedom. This is tragically becoming the only imaginable way in the American mind. I am saddened to say this, but we have neglected peace education for so long that it is difficult for Americans to comprehend peace as anything but a pause in war. War remains the dominant way of being in the world.

This is precisely why I am heartened to learn how SGI women exert themselves wholeheartedly and tirelessly in promoting peace cultures. And it is not simply women of one generation. The SGI young women are invaluable, for who better than they to speak to those their own age about the vitality and practicality of peace. I am grateful for the work done by the SGI women, and when two of my students recently were awarded one of the Kathryn W. Davis 100 Projects for Peace, I immediately contacted the SGI women. These students will be creating a documentary for use in American high schools and colleges to educate young Americans about the bombing of Nagasaki.

A Woman's Vow

IKEDA: Your students are taking action for peace based on your inspiration—a wonderful example of the triumph of education. Emerson was also, again, keenly aware of women's formidable innate capacities for empathy, dialogue, and culture.

On June 13, 1996, I delivered a commemorative address titled "Thoughts on Education for Global Citizenship" at Teachers College, Columbia University, in New York. I enumerated three conditions for the global citizenship so urgently needed today:

(1) The wisdom to perceive the interconnectedness of all life and living.

(2) The courage not to fear or deny difference but to respect and strive to understand people of different cultures and to grow from encounters with them.

(3) The compassion to maintain an imaginative empathy that reaches beyond one's immediate surroundings and extends to those suffering in distant places.[7]

I believe that all three of these are areas in which women can play a larger role.

As I shared in my speech, there is a Buddhist scripture that tells the story of such a woman. Queen Shrimala, a contemporary of Shakyamuni, is described in the sutra bearing her name as making this vow:

If I see lonely people, people who have been jailed unjustly and have lost their freedom, people who are suffering from

illness, disaster or poverty, I will not abandon them. I will
bring them spiritual and material comfort.[8]

And, the sutra tells us, she faithfully observed this vow throughout her life.

WIDER: By attending to actual circumstances, Queen Shrimala
met people where they were. Her strength as a woman and her
deeply compassionate affection shaped her every act.

Your conditions for global citizenship speak eloquently to the
central task facing us in the twenty-first century. Each condition is
equally important in extending our perception of profound interconnection into every action. On the occasion of my 2006 visit to
Soka Women's College, I had this to say about the role of women:
"We all know that there is more that fundamentally unites us than
divides us, and as women I think we are particularly poised to
do the hard work in the world to bring forth those fundamental
connections."

IKEDA: The same year, in November 2006, I met Betty Williams,
Nobel Peace Prize laureate and president and founder of the World
Centers of Compassion for Children International. In 1976, in
Northern Ireland, where strife had raged for many years, she stood
boldly with other housewives and friends, and, with the strength
of grassroots solidarity, launched what is called the Great Peace
March. Since then, she has worked for the protection of women
and children on the global stage.

At first, some people mocked her and her movement as nothing
but ignorant women. She also felt guilty when she was forced to
leave her children at home under someone else's care, so she could
take part in activities. I still remember her candidly telling me:

There were days when I think, "I'm tired," when I think,
"I can't go on any longer. . . ." My children sometimes said

to me, "Mother, why do you have to leave us and go to participate in your activities for peace?"

She added with humor, "Now, my grandchildren are saying the same thing."

Overcoming the challenges and difficulties presented by the demands of daily life and taking action for world peace and the betterment of society is, to me, both noble and admirable.

WIDER: We must encourage children to think big, so that they may see how their own mothers matter to others. Here is a case in point involving Betty Williams herself: When I had just graduated from high school, I was given the marvelous opportunity to hear her and her coworker Mairead Corrigan. I was deeply inspired by their unwavering dedication to peace. Until now, I've never had the chance to express how powerful it was to hear them. At the time, even with all the peace work of the 1960s, violence remained the unquestioned center in so many areas of discussion.

Betty Williams and Mairead Corrigan took us to a different reality. The notes I took then speak for all time: Mairead Corrigan advocated for "peaceful change of that which is wrong," encouraging us all to "stretch out the hand of friendship." Betty Williams reminded us how "war is always wrong," bringing home that reality by telling us what happens under conditions of war: "Our children learn nothing but violence." They laid one of the foundation stones in my own daily work in building cultures of peace. How vital is their message to all the world's adults.

IKEDA: Thank you for sharing these precious memories. They are important testimony, shining with a profound philosophy of peace.

As she revealed in our discussion, Betty Williams has been courageous in her struggle as a mother: "My son said: 'Today, Mommy, I'm just beginning to realize, because of this situation in the world now, what you did when we were younger, you fought to save my life so that I wouldn't die.'"[9] I feel sure that these words from her son are her greatest joy, pride, and supreme honor.

Mrs. Williams has warmly encouraged the activities of Soka women:

> The women of the Soka Gakkai are part of a spiritual network of women around the world contributing to peace. Comprised of mothers who are the nurturers of life, this network is one of shared understanding.[10]

I am certain that the courageous, compassionate joint efforts of women to build a peaceful world and a society shining with happiness for all will have positive effects in communities around the world and lead the history of the twenty-first century in a new, better direction.

CONVERSATION TWELVE

To Open All Doors

IKEDA: In about 1860, Masaoki Shinmi and a delegation from the Edo shogunate traveled to Washington, D.C., for a meeting with President James Buchanan and the ratification of the U.S.-Japan Treaty of Amity and Commerce. The delegation then traveled to New York, where the people enthusiastically welcomed them. Broadway was lined with tens of thousands eager to watch them parade past in carriages accompanied by an honor guard.

A member of the throng, Walt Whitman later shared his impressions:

> *Over the Western sea hither from Niphon come,*
> *Courteous, the swart-cheek'd two-sworded envoys,*
> *Leaning back in their open barouches, bare-headed,*
> > *impassive,*
> *Ride to-day through Manhattan.*[1]

No doubt the members of the delegation were heartened by this warm public reception.

I first visited New York in October 1960, a century after

Whitman composed these lines. I had just become the third Soka Gakkai president (May 3, 1960). I remember visiting the United Nations Headquarters and reaffirming my vow to further the cause of world peace. The independence of a growing number of African nations was a breath of fresh air for the United Nations. The sight of the youthful representatives of newly independent African nations left a deep impression on me, and it was on this occasion that I declared the twenty-first century would be the Century of Africa.

WIDER: Whitman's words evoke his beloved Manhattan as the great meeting place of the world. How fitting that your first visit to New York marked the centennial of that auspicious occasion.

IKEDA: The celebrated author Soseki Natsume first introduced Walt Whitman to Japanese readers. Since that time, many other famous Japanese thinkers and cultural leaders, such as Kanzo Uchimura, Takeo Arishima, and Shiko Munakata, have been fond of his poetry. Many of them, including Saika Tomita and Seigo Shirotori, whose translations of *Leaves of Grass* I loved, were poets of the populist group the Poets of Democracy in Japan.

In the American movie *Dead Poets Society* (1989), which was also popular in Japan, a new teacher uses Whitman's poetry to appeal directly to the students' feelings and open their hearts and minds.

What is the current American evaluation of Whitman?

WIDER: In the world of American literary scholarship, he is a powerful figure known for his groundbreaking poetry. He can also be seen as someone who advocated for an inclusive democracy. He is, you can say, the heart of democracy at the heart of the United States.

But if you were to ask people in school or on the street to talk about Walt Whitman, a lot of times I think you would get a blank stare. In the United States at large, a culture of poetry has rarely been affirmed. However, poetry remains strong in many communities, especially now with the Spoken Word Movement, in which I think Whitman would be active were he alive today.

Those who know Whitman's work regard him as the person who changed the face of American poetry. Inspired by Emerson, he broke away from rule-bound forms, opening poetry to all different voices.

And yet, for all his inclusiveness, Whitman, too, betrays his limits. As many have noted, his perspective is heavily male, and his comments about the United States can sound jingoistic. He certainly participated in some of the prejudices of the time, even as he imagined the possibility for a vibrant inclusivity, where humanity is valued for all its complex ways of being in the world.

IKEDA: Yes, of course you're right. You comment on the small scale of poetry culture in American society; the same is true in Japan. The enjoyment of the wonders of poetry is not a part of most people's daily lives.

As Whitman wrote, "The words of the true poems give you more than poems."[2] We should strive to create a society that exhibits the vibrant power of poetry and glows with the poetic spirit.

You participated, Dr. Wider, in the scholarly symposium on Whitman in 2005 at the Ikeda Center for Peace, Learning, and Dialogue. In discussing the role required of poets today, you mentioned Whitman's conviction that poetry has the power to open all doors.

WIDER: There I had the opportunity to discuss the power of poetry in its broadest application. I love the derivation of the English word for *poetry*. It comes from a Greek word meaning "to make" or "to do." It's a hands-on word, suggesting how active poetry is. Active and creative.

In our current societies, where conflict and violence-based

solutions dominate, poets face profound challenges. How do we directly address violence without sacrificing our voices to violence-based rhetoric? How do we speak a common language and yet make that language transformative, so that it does not perpetuate the violence it seeks to abate?

History amply demonstrates the power of poetry in violent times. People like Gandhi, Martin Luther King Jr., Marilyn Buck, and Leonard Peltier have kept the flame of poetry burning brightly even when confined to the dark world of prison. This was true of Tsunesaburo Makiguchi and Josei Toda as well.

And today, look at the poetry gatherings that persist, despite overbearing violence. In Iraq, Yanar Mohammed, co-founder of the Organization of Women's Freedom in Iraq, creates Freedom Space for poetry.[3] In the United States, I think of the ongoing work by Sam Hamill and many others through Poets Against the War.[4]

Today's seeming independence through individualism is illusory. Often it is nothing more than isolation and indifference. In an increasingly mechanized world, we have learned to think of ourselves as parts of a machine unaware of how each works with the other.

Whitman's beloved image of the grass is instructive and heartening. Grass grows throughout the world: in the desert, in the plains, in marshes, in tundra. Whitman knew how common grass was. And look at its strength. While we can distinctly see each blade, each is nonetheless connected by an intricate root system that makes its life and growth possible. The grass grows from the earth, where it touches everyone and is touched by everyone. Through his metaphor, Whitman asks us to be so attentive that we see the single blade while at the same time perceive our fundamental interconnectedness with all others and with the world itself.

His poetry provides our means for understanding. Here poetry is both at work and at home. The poetic spirit resides in this power to communicate a fundamental and profound perception, in which many can share and participate. Your poetry is the very model of this spirit.

CRYSTALLIZATION OF THE BOND

IKEDA: You praise me too highly. I am moved and inspired by your description of the "leaves of grass" as a symbol of the interconnectedness of the vast world.

Nichiren wrote:

> When spring comes and conditions of wind and rain prevail, then even the mindless plants and trees will all put forth buds, blossom in glory, and make their presence known to the world. And when the autumn arrives with its conditions of autumn moonlight, then plants and trees will all ripen and bear fruit. Then they will nourish all sentient beings, sustain their lives, bring them to maturity, and in the end manifest both the virtue and the functions of Buddhahood.[5]

This passage urges us to awaken to the profundity of human existence in explaining that even plants and trees, through their interconnections with all other things, manifest wondrous compassion and power.

I agree with you that the "poetic spirit resides in this power to communicate a fundamental and profound perception, in which many can share and participate." Truly moving poetry goes beyond expressing feelings and emotions. Essentially, it is a crystallization of the bond between individuals, between people and society, and between humanity and nature. In strengthening these bonds and connections, it maximizes the potential of each individual and becomes a source of light making the worth and dignity of the individual shine their brightest.

The works of great poets like Hugo, Tagore, Byron, and Pushkin overflow with this integrating power. Whitman's poetry continues to shine today as an example of such poetry.

I was invited to the ceremony held in March 1992 in Camden, New Jersey, to mark the centennial of Whitman's death. Though I wasn't able to attend, I contributed a poem titled "Like the Sun Rising," in which I praised Whitman as a poet of the people:

> *No one is another's master*
> *no one another's slave—*
> *politics, learning, religion, art*
> *all exist for the human being*
> *for the sake of the people.*
> *To undo the prejudice of race,*
> *to break down the walls of class,*
> *to share freedom and equality with the people—*
> *it is for this that you sing*
> *to the last limits of your strength.*
>
> *Your songs—*
> *the Declaration of Humanity*
> *for a new age.*
>
> *You are the greatest lover*
> *of the common people,*
> *are yourself one*
> *of the proud uncrowned mass*
> *throughout your life.*[6]

WIDER: Powerful words. Whitman would have been honored by them. As you say so aptly, he was the "greatest lover / of the common people." He championed the powerful comrades of freedom

and equality, and fundamentally opposed all distinctions that clas-
sified some as superior, others as inferior.

His poems speak beautifully for his commitment. For example,
consider the language he used in his poems. At the time, poetic
language was considered a "special" language, far different from
the patterns of everyday speech. Whitman, however, wrote using
the language of the people, the language of the street, the language
in daily use. He wanted his poetry to sound like daily life.

IKEDA: The vibrant sounds of daily life are the lifeline of the
poet of the people. I am reminded of words of the historian Johan
Huizinga to the effect that the pathos of democracy is to be found
nowhere more strongly than in the poetic texts of Walt Whitman.
Indeed, Whitman's poems pulsate with the soul of democracy and
a paean to the people. Whitman wrote, "Our American superiority and vitality are in the bulk of our people, not in a gentry like
the old world."[7] Clearly Whitman believed that throwing oneself
into the sea of the people is the way to growth and development
as a poet.

WIDER: Going hand in hand with his choice of language is his
choice of material. The two are, of course, integrally related.
Our language reflects our experience; our experience shapes our
language.

As did Emerson, Whitman felt that poetry was boundless. No
subject was unfit. Whitman wanted to include everything and everyone in his poems. Again, this contrasted with the perceived
wisdom of the day, where seamstresses', factory workers', slaves' experiences did not appear in poems unless these experiences were
romanticized or presented at arm's length. Whitman included human beings of all experiences in his poems as living persons and
not as literary devices.

TODA UNIVERSITY

IKEDA: The ordinary people, courageously leading their lives in the face of innumerable obstacles, were his subject and focus. He wrote, "Other writers [poets] look on a laborer as a laborer, a poet as a poet, a President as a President, a merchant as a merchant—and so on."[8] But Whitman himself "looks on the President as a man, on the laborer as a man—on the poet and all the rest, as a man."[9] He was indeed a poet who saw and lauded a man as a man, a poet for whom the title *poet of the people* was the supreme honor.

Born and brought up in a poor household, he started working when only eleven years old. He gained practical wisdom and grew and learned from his varied experiences as a printer, typesetter, substitute primary-school teacher, and journalist. He wrote gratefully about his good fortune in working with fine newspaper editors: "There you get your culture direct: not through borrowed source—no, a century of college training could not confer such results on anyone."[10]

His words express my own feelings of gratitude for the experience I gained working under Josei Toda and the wide-ranging instruction he provided me. In the days of turmoil following the end of World War II, I decided to give up the night-school classes I had been attending to lend my support to Mr. Toda's troubled businesses. Promising to give me a full education through private lessons, Mr. Toda instructed me in politics, economics, law, history, Chinese literature, chemistry, physics, and astronomy for ten years, up to the time of his death. I remember him smiling broadly and saying, "Let's just call it Toda University."

Once when we were discussing Whitman, I recited a passage from the poem "Pioneers, O Pioneers" for him. I still remember him saying, after listening intently: "Right! No matter what happens, we are on the march. I'm advancing. You advance, too. Forward, always forward!"

In spite of the adverse circumstances we were battling, he once, after finishing a lecture, took a flower from a vase on his desk and, placing it in my breast pocket, said, "A prize for being my star pupil!" Though it was a mere flower, it felt to me like the greatest medal from my mentor. We had no buildings or campus, but I was convinced that Toda University was the best university in the world. I made up my mind that, after graduating, I would dedicate my life to promoting Mr. Toda's vision to the world as his inseparable, loyal disciple.

WIDER: The depth of the mentor-disciple bond between the two of you moves me profoundly as does Mr. Toda's use of Whitman's poetry to encourage you to learn, develop, and grow in every circumstance. His beautiful and powerful response in poetry is so fitting given how integral the poetic response of one person to another was to Whitman.

You and Whitman are indeed kindred spirits. You, too, raise sonorous praise for the people. I think of these lines from "The People":

> From the beginning
> there's been nothing to surpass the strength and shout of the
>   people
> from the beginning
> nothing to outrun the pace of the people's wisdom
> from the beginning
> nothing to rival the banners of the people's justice[11]

One of the elements that I so value in your poetry is your way of including your readers. You enable us to feel the immediate present and thus become part of what is happening within the poem. Whitman would have been delighted. He, too, wanted people to read themselves into his poems; he wanted no one left out.

The way a poem affects a person is crucial. However, it is a two-way street. We must also let ourselves be affected by the poem.

IKEDA: There is no doubt that the revival of the poetic spirit is essential today. I am especially eager for younger generations to inherit the vigorous spirituality of poetry, and this is why I often share words of the world's great poets, such as Whitman, at entrance and graduation ceremonies at Soka University of America and other Soka schools. For example, in my address at the entrance ceremony of Soka University of Japan in the spring of 2010, I quoted a passage from the work of the Armenian poet Yeghishe Charents:

> Brilliant victory for your spring!
> Your path is already strewn with flowers.
> It is you yourselves who will turn that path to gold[12]

I then encouraged the incoming students to strive together to create a golden record of achievement and remain positive in the face of every challenge, offering my sincere congratulations on their wonderful new beginning.

WIDER: What better way to begin their university journey than through poetry. Truly, yours are campuses for the poetic heart. The very places bespeak the spirit in which students are invited to engage in study. We have already mentioned the statues of poets like Tagore and Hugo on the Soka University campus. I also love the statue where Whitman, left hand aloft, gazes in wonder at the butterfly that has seemingly just landed on his outstretched hand. While statues often mute personality or make famous people seem unapproachable, those on the Soka campuses invite us to respond. Eminently approachable, none are cordoned off by fence. They are poetry in another form.

LIBERATING GODS

IKEDA: We have a statue at the Kansai Soka Junior and Senior High Schools, too. I hope someday soon you can see it with our students. It has Whitman, hat in hand, striding forth calmly. On its installation, I quoted a Whitman verse that I have treasured since my youth:

> *Allons! through struggles and wars!*
> *The goal that was named cannot be countermanded.*[13]

WIDER: I look forward to seeing the statue someday. I think how often in the United States we erect statues of military or political leaders. Instead, what if we commemorated those who contributed to the arts and built cultures of peace? I feel strongly that our poets have been the most courageous people: those with the ability to voice what has been silenced. When a community of people is being denied its voice, the poet is the person who can speak.

Especially nowadays, when violence silences those who suffer most, I celebrate the poets who continue to speak and to act on their words. For example, Omékongo Dibinga travels the world to bring education to life through poetry. Congolese, he now lives in the United States, where he can work most effectively: leading educational workshops, participating in poetry gatherings, and addressing people everywhere about the horrific violence in the Democratic Republic of the Congo. Where women are often silenced as a statistic or inhumanely considered the war's "collateral damage," he speaks directly to what these women experience so that those of us who hear may act on the reality of suffering rather than on its disguise.

When Emerson talked about poets, he used a phrase that I have always loved. He called poets liberating gods. First, put the emphasis where the phrase ends. What does it mean to call poets "gods"? It sounds dangerous, attributing omnipotence to human beings. However, if you understand Emerson's use of the word *god*, you see a different potential: a poet embodies a distinctly creative power not as an isolated individual but as a larger expression of the unifying Over-Soul.

Then place the emphasis on the word *liberating*, and see how it draws attention to what poets do. They liberate. Poets free others so that they can, in turn, express the creative power that manifests differently within each of us. I think poets are absolutely vital to the health of any community. Not only do they keep the creative power alive within humanity, they encourage its different and varied expressions. If you silence the poets, you silence all of us.

IKEDA: A treasured friend, the South African poet Oswald Mbuyiseni Mtshali, is a man of deep convictions who fought long against apartheid. In May 1991, when I first met him, he related how, in his youth, a woman had taught him that poetry is the means for expressing our fiery passions, vast hopes, and magnificent aspirations.

I asked him when he wrote his first verses. Gazing into the distance, he replied:

> It was a poem to my mother. My mother's death was a great shock to me, so great that I almost couldn't recover from it. It took me a long time to get over it. But eventually, I noticed something. Whatever strength I had was something my mother had given to me, left to me. My mother's words were alive in me; my mother lived on inside me.
>
> When I recognized that, a poem to my mother welled up spontaneously from the depths of my heart. I was moved by something akin to instinct. That first poem was an expression of my deep love for and gratitude to my mother.[14]

Hearing this, I perceived the origin of his poetry.

WIDER: How important it is to understand the source of our poetic expression. In Mr. Mtshali's case, his mother's example and teaching created the strength from which he spoke. Many of us would find this true, no matter what kind of poetry we practice in our lives.

IKEDA: At my suggestion, a Japanese floral arrangement was placed in the room where we met. When he noticed it, I told him it was in memory of his parents' beautiful lives. Delighted, he said, "I feel as if my parents were with me now."

We talked together for two and a half hours without pause. I sympathized with this man who had used poetry, the highest manifestation of the human spirit, to combat apartheid, an infamous crime against humanity.

In times of crisis, it is the poet's role to sound the alarm and awaken the people. Further, it is the mission of the poet to cause the sun of boundless courage and hope to rise in the people's hearts and in this way make peace possible.

At the conclusion of our talk, I extolled his committed efforts:

> Words infused with spirit are everlasting. And please know how valuable your poetry is. I believe that the poetic spirit will revive in the twenty-first century. Unless it does, our souls will suffocate.
>
> The bureaucracies of science, government, and economics are expanding and growing ever more oppressive. Unless this trend is reversed, we will be crushed under their weight.
>
> Poetry expands and liberates the human spirit to an infinite degree. It enriches it. Like music, it transcends

boundaries and divisions and links all human hearts. There is no discrimination in the world of poetry.

During the nearly twenty years since our discussion, my conviction that this is true has steadily strengthened.

Rooted in Dialogue

IKEDA: For humanity, the universe is an eternal frontier. As Emerson said in wonder at the stars, "What perfection and elegancy in them—nothing else in nature has the grandeur and influence upon the mind."[1]

Akatsuki, Japan's unmanned spacecraft formerly known as the Venus Climate Orbiter, was launched in May 2010. It was scheduled to arrive at the planet Venus in December 2010.[2] A microsatellite named *Negai* (Wish), developed by our Soka University Faculty of Engineering, launched with it. Under the guidance of Professor Seiji Kuroki, university students built the satellite using commercially available parts and their own ingenuity. Research and development started in 2003. Since then, in a process of trial and error, the work has been handed down from older to younger students.

Making about 500 orbits of the Earth in a little over a month, the Soka University microsatellite successfully conducted experiments in advanced data processing under the harsh conditions of space. When its mission was complete, as a finale, it entered the atmosphere, blazing as a beautiful shooting star.

The *Negai* carried a hope-giving cargo in the form of microfilms of postcards conveying the wishes (*negai*) of eight thousand children. Some of these messages expressed dreams of becoming teachers or astronomers. Some expressed longing for a world free of war.

It received extensive media coverage as a project designed to encourage and inspire children, and it garnered a positive public response. Originated by students, the concept has been praised as a plan worthy of Soka University, an institution of the highest ideals of humane education.

WIDER: When the children sent their messages on that aptly named satellite, they launched poems into the far-reaching expanses. What are dreams and longings but other forms of poetry? Those who made room for children's voices on *Negai* live out the poetic spirit in their willingness to make connections and listen to others' wishes. The process by which the satellite was created speaks to this—collaborative work, in which many take part. Certainly this is a poem of and from the people.

IKEDA: Since 2000, the Kansai Soka Junior and Senior High Schools have been participating in the NASA educational outreach program Earth Knowledge Acquired by Middle School Students, or EarthKAM, which involves remote-controlled photography of the Earth.[3] They have established the world's record in program participation (thirty-two times) and in 2008 were awarded first prize in the climate-change-analysis mission.

The year 2010, by the way, marked the eightieth anniversary of Soka education, and the Soka Junior and Senior High Schools were founded forty-three years ago. By 2011, forty years had passed since the founding of Soka University, in 1971. As founder, I hope these institutions will continue to further cultivate wise students who can contribute to peace and happiness from the cosmos-embracing viewpoint represented by these activities.

I understand that Colgate University celebrated its 190th anniversary in 2009. With this venerable tradition, it is ranked high among universities in the United States. I would be most interested to learn more of its history and current projects.

WIDER: Colgate University was founded in 1819 as a religious institution, at that time open only to men. It was affiliated with the Baptist Church and designed to educate young men to become ministers.

The early school was small. The story goes that it was founded by thirteen men with thirteen prayers and thirteen dollars. Our oldest buildings on campus were built by these first faculty and students working together. They are dorms now, and one houses the Women's Studies Center on the ground floor. I teach in this building. It is good to have women's studies literally as the foundation of one of the oldest buildings on campus.

Colgate remained a Baptist institution for some years. Finally, the theological seminary separated and went its own way and is now in Rochester, New York. Colgate University has been a small liberal-arts college, as it is now, since the late nineteenth century.

IKEDA: The founding, building, and development of a university are sources of social betterment. I can imagine the great conviction and hard work of the pioneers who created your university. I know they would be proud if they could see how wonderfully it has developed.

Charles William Eliot, who served as Harvard University president for about forty years and is known as the father of modern Harvard, said, "Universities are among the most permanent of human institutions."⁴ This is why their existence is so significant and valuable to society.

But creating a university, putting it on track, building its tradition, and keeping it going demand tremendous efforts. Actually acquiring the land and engaging faculty members for the opening of Soka University of Japan presented a whole series of difficulties. And government permission, needed to begin enrollment, was only received three months before the scheduled opening. Even so, more than 7,800 applicants—a figure far higher than we had anticipated—took the entrance examinations. Though delighted and gratified, I was extremely disappointed, too, because the limited number of spaces available meant that some applicants had to be turned down.

Even after the school opened, we bore in mind the truth that construction requires tenacious, painstaking effort, while destruction takes but an instant. In the hope of helping Soka University develop, I traveled to such noted institutions as Cambridge, Oxford, and the Sorbonne to study the best elements of their traditions.

What has been considered especially important by Colgate faculty members for students' training and education?

WIDER: Colgate has worked very hard to create the best physical space for students to learn in. One important thing is the physical campus itself and the kind of facilities offered to the students—the labs, the classrooms, the athletic facilities, the living facilities.

We've also worked very hard to assemble a faculty that represents many areas of expertise. We need to be thoroughly grounded in our own fields and yet able to work with students still in the early stages of their intellectual journeys. At Colgate, commitment to ideals means that the students and the faculty work closely together.

In 2010, we welcomed our sixteenth president, Jeffrey Herbst. He has encouraged the students to understand three elements essential for their college learning: to work closely with faculty on research; to understand how, even while still *in* and *at* college, education extends beyond a college campus; and thus to get involved in service-learning and take part in off-campus study programs.

IKEDA: Emphasizing liberal arts education and faculty members' fields of expertise, generating a spirit of close cooperation between faculty and students, and promoting community service and extra-curricular activities—these are all areas in which both Soka University of Japan and Soka University of America can and should learn much.

I understand that your lectures are popular among the students.

WIDER: In a word, I love teaching. There is nothing better than a semester-long dialogue with the people in my classes—unless it's when the dialogue continues across classes and indeed beyond the four short years of undergraduate education.

Conversation and dialogue are elemental to human beings. We don't live well or fully if we cannot share our thoughts and feelings with others. Inquiry, examination, and collaboration are central to this sharing.

Seats are sometimes hard to come by in my classrooms; I am fortunate that many students want to take my classes. At present, I teach courses in several fields, a variety I both delight in and feel is important to my ongoing intellectual growth. In addition to nineteenth-century American literature, I teach many courses in the women's studies program: introduction to women's studies, which is a cross-disciplinary course, as well as courses specifically in literature—including women's biography and autobiography, and novels featuring women as central characters.

Another area in the curriculum I've developed at Colgate is con-temporary Native American literature, in which I currently teach many courses. Partly because of the very nature of the liberal-arts college and partly because we want to keep broadening the cur-riculum to open as many thought-provoking doors to our students as possible, I have been encouraged to develop new courses. I am currently contemplating a course on poet-activists Adrienne Rich and Audre Lorde.

IKEDA: Your words convey the spirit of opening fresh and exciting new vistas of learning. I agree that teaching well means learning well. Moreover, in the years to come, free-spirited, innovative universities with flexible curricula to meet the needs of the changing times will become increasingly important.

At present, what are the main ways that your women's studies have expanded, in what areas?

WIDER: In addition to offering more sections of the introduction to women's studies course, we have added courses in various areas: feminist rhetorics and social change; women and religious thought; women, health and medicine. We also are now the sponsoring program for a minor in lesbian, gay, bisexual, transgender, and queer studies.

Over the last few years, the introductory women's studies courses have grown larger and larger. Sections can easily rise to forty students each, which is large for Colgate, where effort is made to limit classes to twenty-five. Still I find it difficult to exclude students from a class they want to take. Now we routinely run two sections each semester.

In class, I see us all engaged in a shared journey. As we travel, we converse. We think together. In the best situations, interpretations rise, like a strong and well-built structure, through the marvelous process of dialogue, built upon the strength of multiple perspectives. We'll often create time to meet at one of our coffee houses to converse in a different setting. And this semester, one of my students is pursuing an independent study on conversation itself. My classes, you might say, are rooted in dialogue.

IKEDA: I can see why your classes are popular. In the true Platonic spirit, you employ every opportunity for dialogue to share your students' quest for truth.

Respect, Encouragement, Appreciation

WIDER: So often students have learned during their schooling to repeat a well-received interpretation or to say what they think the teacher wants to hear. I want my students to think freely and fully, to examine carefully what they have come to think and how they have arrived at their ideas and understandings. I believe there is nothing more important than mutual and compassionate respect between teacher and student.

I bring in the word *compassionate*, because respect can also be associated with fear or with dispassion. Both stand in the way of true learning. If we fear our teachers, there is a great danger that we will seek to mimic them rather than develop our own creative intellect. If we feel we must maintain an objectivity that distances people from one another, we are likely to treat learning as no more than a mind game, in which the outcome doesn't matter.

IKEDA: You have touched on a major issue. Buddhism stresses the importance of true dialogue as a meeting of minds, presenting its teachings in the form of dialogues between a mentor and disciple. And you emphasize the importance of consideration and respect in dialogue.

These are values consonant with the four methods employed by bodhisattvas in Mahayana Buddhism. These four methods are qualities conducive to creating ideal interpersonal relations. The first is selfless almsgiving, including spiritual nourishment, courage, and other nonmaterial support. The second is loving speech, or speaking in a kindly manner. The third is altruistic action, taking action to benefit others. And the fourth is shared efforts— working together with others.

By practicing these four kinds of conduct, one respects the other person, improves the relationship, promotes mutual growth, and uplifts both parties. This is the spirit in which you, Dr. Wider, interact with, encourage, and pursue the truth with your students. They are fortunate to have you for a teacher.

WIDER: In class, I begin from the premise of respect. How can we learn if we don't treat one another with dignity and interest? We each and all deserve respect for our insights, our concerns, and our questions. Every stage of life holds its own distinct perspectives, and wherever life finds us, we are wise if we remember to listen.

IKEDA: Great educators are always modest. Your delight at exchanges of opinion with students and your eagerness to learn things with them are most moving. Listening and lending an ear—these open the heart and show respect for the other person, in turn generating mutual inspiration and spurring creativity.

Such an attitude was pivotal to Emerson's educational philosophy. He wrote, "But they [universities] can only highly serve us when they aim not to drill, but to create; when they gather from far every ray of various genius to their hospitable halls, and by the concentrated fires, set the hearts of their youth on flame."[5] Emerson believed that the aim of education is to build character and to help young people manifest their full potential. Convinced that universities should gather and protect all kinds of genius, he vigorously opposed any teaching that forced young people into established molds or constrained and repressed them. He believed the ideal teacher to be one who, through conversation and interaction, sets the hearts of youth on fire.

Nichiren, quoting the classical Chinese work *Xunzi*, used the expression, "From the indigo, an even deeper blue."[6] While the blue dye comes from indigo, when something is repeatedly dyed in it, the color becomes deeper than that of the indigo plant. This expresses the need for the teacher to strive to educate his or her students to surpass him or her and the concomitant need of the students to respond to their teacher's dedication by striving their hardest as well. It bespeaks a true unity of teacher and student in the learning process. This is very similar to Emerson's views and, indeed, should be a universal guidepost for education.

President Makiguchi treasured this expression and proclaimed the same conviction himself:

> The ideal for a teacher who is determined to be the best leader possible is to guide his students to becoming the best kind of human beings, even though they surpass him.
>
> Teachers should come down from the throne where they are ensconced as the objects of veneration to become public servants who offer guidance to those who seek to ascend to the throne of learning. They should not be masters who offer themselves as paragons, but partners in the discovery of new models.[7]

The mission and responsibility of teachers are to believe firmly in the potential of each student and to exert themselves to the utmost to make each student surpass them.

WIDER: Your words enable me to understand why students receiving Soka education—at Soka University and Soka Women's College in Japan and at Soka University of America—are so strongly motivated and active. Visiting these three institutions, I have seen firsthand the true attentiveness schools practicing Soka education devote to each of their students.

It seems to me that Soka education works with a deep understanding of how learning takes place in the individual. Respect is essential. You see this respect manifested in the encouragement students receive from the faculty members and from you. It's an empowering encouragement, not simply a pat on the head or a vague positive comment. It speaks specifically to the individuals, addressing their needs at the moment—both the strength they embody and the obstacles they face. It reminds them of strength in achievement and also shows what more they still can do.

The other quality is appreciation. True appreciation is a rare gem, though it may lie unpolished within us. It is certainly not to be confused with praise or approval; it stems from deep consideration.

IKEDA: It is vital to appreciate students' efforts with both affection and accuracy. Young people are keenly aware of how they are being evaluated. They can accept even severe criticism if they know it is fair and based on genuine care and concern, if it is meant as fuel for growth and improvement. Like everyone else, students derive great security and self-confidence from the awareness that someone knows them well and appreciates them accurately. In this sense, it is impossible to overemphasize the importance of what you mean by appreciation.

WIDER: Appreciation requires us to speak with measured and forthright detail about people, their work, who they are, and what they do. It creates circumstances in which people not only learn more readily but also are more willing to take risks in their intellectual growth.

It is much easier to venture into the unknown when you feel that nobody is going to judge you harshly. If your work doesn't come out exactly as you would have liked, others are going to help you figure out why something didn't succeed, rather than criticize you for taking a risk. Collaboration takes the place of judgment.

Such appreciation is not consistently part of the American system, whether in business, sports, education, or healthcare. The emphases on product over process and on competition at all costs hit home. As my students tell me, if you don't keep pushing for yourself, the competition will beat you out. There is no time to think; certainly no time to think differently. Competition to win takes precedence. And when competition becomes an end in itself, we seem to have no time for the hard work of appreciation. Or I should say, we rarely take time.

Time is always there, if we choose to understand its real presence. What is this real presence? Remember any moment when you chose to listen to someone even though you had no time, or when you were so engrossed in an activity that markings on a clock became meaningless, or when you looked at a cliffside and realized its deep, long history: Then you will know the real presence of time.

Nowadays, instead of appreciation, we follow a different system that demands immediate results. All too often in conversation with my students, I hear how, again and again, they have felt ridiculed or belittled when they took risks. They weren't given the time for the often slow work of innovation. In my own classes, I have tried to emulate Soka education, where risk-taking, creativity, and innovation are encouraged.

IKEDA: Respect, encouragement, and appreciation are fundamental conditions for the practice of outstanding humane education. And thank you again for your warm, deep understanding of Soka education.

I spoke with Victor A. Sadovnichy, the rector of Moscow State University, about the importance of the teacher-student relationship.[8] This one-on-one relationship is the seed for positive growth, we agreed. As a result, the teacher has a very important role to play. A school is not a building—it is an edifice constructed of its educators' character.

The first step in education is to believe in students' potential. This must be the starting point for all educators.

Both presidents Makiguchi and Toda were model practitioners of the three points you mention: respect, encouragement, and appreciation. This deep commitment to compassion and action are the starting points of Soka education and the pedagogic ideal for which we strive.

Learning Journeys

IKEDA: Education is a holy calling transcending generations to be passed from the past to the present and into the future. In this conversation, I want to discuss further with you the path it ought to follow in the twenty-first century.

WIDER: November 2010 marked the eightieth anniversary of Soka education. I understand it was born from the mentor-disciple relationship between Tsunesaburo Makiguchi and Josei Toda. No wonder the mentor-disciple relationship is the heartbeat of this educational method or, more aptly, way of life.

Designed to cultivate the distinct potential of each student, Soka education so clearly understands the importance of person-to-person engagement. Only then can new values emerge and humane reforms be undertaken.

We learn best when we are responsible to one another. We each need a person further along in life, more knowledgeable as well as comfortably honest and unpretentious, who can know us well enough to challenge, guide, encourage, and help provide the thought-provoking "maps" for our own learning journeys.

IKEDA: The essence of education is the stimulation and inspiration provided by the relationship between teacher and student. This is why it's impossible to discuss Soka education without discussing the solemn mentor-and-disciple relationship.

President Makiguchi had many years' practical experience in primary schools, as both a teacher and principal. In the process, he evolved his pedagogic theories, which, through the concerted efforts of his disciple, Josei Toda, were assembled as *Soka kyoikugaku taikei* (The System of Value-Creating Pedagogy). The publication date (November 18, 1930) of this great work, a crystallization of mentor-disciple unity, is regarded as the starting point of the Soka Gakkai, which was known at the time as the Soka Kyoiku Gakkai (Value-Creating Education Society).

What is the purpose of Soka education? In "The Theory of Soka Education," Makiguchi stressed the role that education must play in opening the way to peace and happiness for humanity:

> Educational efforts built on a clear understanding and with a defined sense of purpose have the power to overcome the contradictions and doubts that plague humankind and to bring about an eternal victory for humanity.[1]

WIDER: He clarified the vast scope of education's mission and the importance of its founding principles.

IKEDA: Makiguchi entrusted the dream of creating schools for this kind of education to Josei Toda. He told his family often that in the future there would be schools, from kindergarten to university, to put Soka educational theories into practice, and that Toda was sure to fulfill the task of creating them.

As I shall never forget, President Toda told me of Mr. Makiguchi's ideas more than sixty years ago, in November 1950. Although his business affairs were in a terrible condition, his gaze was calmly fixed on the future with a vision as bright and clear as a bracing autumnal sky.

"Daisaku," he said to me, "we've got to create a Soka university. If it can't be done in my lifetime, I leave the task up to you to complete!" Then, looking me in the eye, he added, "And it's got to be the best university in the world." I vowed to realize his vision.

Unlike Mr. Makiguchi and Mr. Toda, I have never been a teacher. Still, I regard carrying on their ideas, by opening Soka education institutions, to be my mission as their true disciple. Over two decades later, in 1971, the centennial of Mr. Makiguchi's birth, Soka University was established. Opening ceremonies took place on April 2, the anniversary of Mr. Toda's death.

After founding the Soka Junior and Senior High Schools and Soka University, I resolutely vowed that I would always look after the students who come to our institutions of learning, no matter what challenges or adversities they might face. This is the attitude a founder must have.

Every day, my wife and I continue to pray for the health and happiness of all our students, both those currently enrolled and alumni. We keep collections of their school essays close at hand, looking through them from time to time, asking how each of them is now, offering words of encouragement.

WIDER: Once again, I am moved by your abiding consideration for the well-being of your students: the deep and inspired thoughts that led you to found the Soka schools, the way you and Mrs. Ikeda maintain contact with your students, and the three-generational bond from Mr. Makiguchi to Mr. Toda to yourself that was the starting point and has become the strong foundation of Soka education.

To add to what I have already said about the characteristics of Soka University of Japan and Soka University of America, your students work with beautiful ambition. I mean this in the purest sense of the word. Their ambition is not ego-driven but founded in the desire to contribute good to this world.

IKEDA: Great ambitions lead to a great life. I believe that the essence of education is drawing this great ambition out of students and enabling them to exercise their full powers.

WIDER: Soka students seem so grounded and so centered. I am reminded of the derivation for the English word *humility*—from *humus*, of the soil. No wonder they are grounded: They act with and from humility, literally from our connection with the earth. This connection is profound and must be deeply honored, especially since modern societies have faltered gravely in their environmental wisdom.

Of course, there will always be some uneasiness about what to do when school is over. Every student faces this situation. A university is like a home, and once you leave this home, you wonder what the world beyond school is going to be like. Yet at their best, universities provide a true home for their students—not a retreat from the rest of the world but a place for thoughtful connection with communities around the world.

Such understanding is prevalent at Soka University of Japan, Soka Women's College, and Soka University of America. Your Soka students pursue their studies with vision. They convey a strong sense of ability to do important work in the world *and* of knowing that one need not wait to engage in this work. They do this work wherever they are and make certain that what they are doing connects and supports the solutions others are creating elsewhere. This impresses me, because when young people understand and act on this understanding, they advance the work for peace and justice with an imagination and energy that are essential to the world's vitality.

IKEDA: As is written in the Chinese classic the *Liji*, or *Book of Rites*, "The good singer makes men (able) to continue his notes, and (so) the good teacher makes them able to carry out his ideas."[2] I am most happy that Soka young people today have so vibrantly inherited the great ambition for peace and humaneness embraced by Makiguchi and Toda. I frequently urge our students to be, as you say, "grounded and centered"—to have a clear purpose.

Soka University came into being at a time of widespread protest on Japanese university campuses, when young people were disillusioned with government and society, and had lost hope for the future. As founder, I wanted to illuminate those dark times with the light of true education. As I mentioned earlier (see Conversation One), I had the following inscriptions engraved on the pedestals of a pair of bronze statues I presented to Soka University at its inception:

> For what purpose should one cultivate wisdom?
> May you always ask yourself this question!
>
> Only labor and devotion to one's mission
> give life its worth.

I arrived at these words only after long, hard thought on the Soka education propounded by Mr. Makiguchi and Mr. Toda. I also had a reason for selecting the sculptures, an angel and a blacksmith and an angel and a printer, once explaining it to a group of freshmen this way:

> The angels soaring into the sky of success represent Soka University students. The smith and the printer represent the nameless masses, whom Soka University students must never forget.

Soka University is an institution for the ordinary people, for the embodiment of their hopes and aspirations. Without awareness of those toiling without recognition, efforts for their welfare remain nothing more than empty dreams. My original purpose was to create a university for the sake of people who cannot attend university. Then as now, I want our students to engrave this in their minds.

MENTAL ALIMENT

WIDER: As an educator myself, I also want to engrave it in my own mind. So often elitism poisons education. The corrosive attitude of "better than" creeps in and destroys community as well as all prospects for life-giving learning. What I think is missing in the United States is the love of education for the immeasurable and true common wealth it brings to our human lives, both individually and communally.

There is something so profoundly satisfying about sharing knowledge. We need our universities and colleges to be yet more inclusive than they are, to honor all ways of knowing and all kinds of learning. In Emerson's words from "The American Scholar," our universities should encourage every student to become a "university of knowledges."[3]

The notion that learning is only good if you can measure it by a fiscal bottom line plagues the United States. American students always find themselves asking, "What kind of job can I get?" or "Is this major going to translate into work?" Oftentimes they feel uncertain about taking on a certain major—theater or philosophy, for instance.

And sadly, parents are often not supportive. Both students and parents fret about how much money they will make in their future careers. I don't want to minimize real monetary needs, but I do want to bring in a practical Thoreauvian perspective.

IKEDA: Thoreau had this candid advice to offer about education in his own time: "We spend more on almost any article of bodily aliment or ailment than on our mental aliment. . . . we did not leave off our education when we begin to be men and women."⁴ We today would do well to heed these words. Education must provide the mental sustenance for personal growth; it must lay the sound foundation for learning that continues throughout life.

Although specialization in subjects suited to the times is important, without sufficient mental and spiritual nourishment, the most brilliant, most materially affluent person will ultimately reach an impasse.

WIDER: Or, as one of my students wisely commented, the reason people accumulate so many material possessions stems from an impoverishment elsewhere in their lives. They acquire things because they are destitute when it comes to true relations. If we encouraged an ethic that valued education for its transformative work, then learning would become heart-, soul-, and mind-satisfying. Such encouragement belongs to all parts of life, from the youngest to the oldest.

What if education meant becoming a leader of culture in your community or becoming a leader of humanism in society? What if, from the earliest grades, school learning was not something to be endured and gotten through but essential to building peace in the world or forwarding the delicate and difficult complexities of creative coexistence with nature? Perhaps then, efforts aimed at good would no longer cause harm.

What if people felt essential within and to the learning process? The fear factor would decline as well, because the importance of their work would no longer depend upon the prestige of a particular grade or a particular job.

IKEDA: It is difficult to put what one learns at university into practice in one's life. Unfortunately, the tendency you describe among your students is widespread in Japan, too.

Along with specialized knowledge, fostering a sense of the purpose and mission of education is increasingly important. This is the source of true purpose and power in life, and this is why I call on the students studying at the Soka education institutions to strive to simultaneously cultivate their intellect, passion, and character, and become well-rounded individuals capable of powerful social contributions.

Numerous educators and intellectuals from many countries have expressed agreement with this ideal. The French art historian René Huyghe put it skillfully when he told me that attaining completeness as a human being requires heightened sensitivity, lucid intelligence, and strong powers of will and discernment. He compared these three elements to the three horses drawing a carriage; the carriage can make no forward progress if any of the three are missing.

WIDER: On the surface, the specialization pursued in many universities seems promising. We focus with precision, we gain more knowledge in a particular subject, and we enter the subject with greater depth. And yet, this also brings limitation.

No one person can achieve such specialization in every field. We run into the danger of which Emerson warned in "The American Scholar":

> The state of society is one in which the members have suffered amputation from the trunk, and strut about so many walking monsters,—a good finger, a neck, a stomach, an elbow, but never a man.[5]

Ideally, we should rely on one another: Our "knowledges" are complementary. But in fact, we don't have (or take) time. There is too little true communication across fields, and thus, instead of deepening us as we hoped specialization would, we grow narrower and narrower. I worry about humanity within societies that reward such intense specialization. It mechanizes us.

When we talk about developing the ability to do something well, we don't mean to the exclusion of other things. Such exclusion turns us into something not quite human and may well cause us to be inhumane in our behaviors. Sadly, it is too easy to forget our responsibility to others when we're involved in an abstract quest for knowledge.

An exclusive focus can become addictive: An idea or a research project becomes our be-all and end-all. Then we start to neglect so much else in our lives. We may well cease even to see the implications of our beloved (and potentially beneficial) research. What started with vision and dedication turns into blinded obsession because of our uncompromising and rigid focus.

OPEN SPACE

IKEDA: The issue you point out is inextricably intertwined with the many threats contemporary society faces. It is a threat to humanity and can easily expand to threaten civilization as a whole. Nothing is more dangerous than knowledge and science running out of control, without ethical guidelines and having lost sight of their true purpose. The development of weapons of mass destruction, such as nuclear arms, is the prime example.

WIDER: Specialization can also diminish human creativity. I think our creativity is at its finest when we are interconnected, so that we can collaborate—with one another, with nature, with the great thoughts of the past, with the great works of art, past and present. Creativity is innate as is the ability to perceive and create connection. Watch any infant in a safe environment, and you will see this amply demonstrated.

However, this creative ability can be damaged, either directly by harsh criticism and ridicule or indirectly when we feel no support for or response to the connections we experience or perceive. When specialization silences our search for relation, it comes at too high a cost.

I am reminded of those horrible experiments in which animals are deprived of light for so long that they lose the power of sight. It's as if to say, if you exclude human beings from a dynamic range of possibilities for too long, they will no longer be able to enter into that larger creativity by which communities and societies work together rather than against one another.

IKEDA: Just such a pitfall lies in wait for education—especially higher education—today. A broad, interdisciplinary education and a commitment to further training and improvement on the part of educators are increasingly important in cultivating a rich humanity and developing creativity. Students who encounter teachers engaged in such efforts are fortunate indeed.

Discussing the true role of liberal arts, the Spanish philosopher José Ortega y Gassett wrote:

> Life is a chaos, a tangled and confused jungle in which man is lost. . . . Culture is what saves human life from being a mere disaster; it is what enables man to live a life which is something above meaningless tragedy or inward disgrace.[6]

As you warned, losing sight of what is most significant to us as human beings deprives us of a compass to guide our lives. Consequently, we must reexamine the essential purpose of the university and higher education. We need to reimagine the purpose of the university and ensure that it develops its full potential.

WIDER: I think the defining qualities of the educated person are compassion, humility, and a real interest in what others know and have experienced. A formal academic degree is not necessarily a measure of education. The people whom I consider most educated are boundlessly interested in life. They know and are fascinated by the world around them. They pay attention and pay respect to where and with whom they are. They want to learn from them, to understand what they think, to appreciate what they know, and to value what they do.

To my mind, those who are educated are always learners. Generosity characterizes them. To be educated means such generosity of spirit that you want to share what you know in an accessible way. Part of this accessibility is making certain you are not taking up all the space—whether the space is measured physically or in openness to others' thoughts and feelings. A generous spirit makes room for others.

Within this open space, the humanely educated person fosters dialogue. Accessibility means exchange of ideas, and true exchange blossoms in the shared collaboration essential to dialogue. Dialogue brings a forward feel to thought and more readily enables thought to be translated into action.

I've seen this in practice at Soka University of America—whether in the annual student-led education conference[7] or in ideas realized in further projects from learning clusters. In every situation, such action arises because there is a profound trust among the students and with their professors.

This rapport—this quality of relation—is elemental to our health as human beings. It is at the heart of the liberal-arts college. Clearly, SUA has taken this deeply to heart.

IKEDA: Founded a decade ago (in 2001), Soka University of America is still young; learning greatly from Colgate's proud tradition of 190 years (founded in 1819), we hope to continue growing and developing.

To our great happiness, *Newsweek* magazine in 2010 ranked

SUA in the top twenty-five of more than 3,000 universities and colleges from across the United States in four categories: most diverse schools, most desirable suburban schools, most desirable small schools, and great schools with great weather. Many graduates and other people connected with the university have expressed their delight at this high evaluation of such a young institution. The encouragement and support provided by you and others who have unbounded faith in SUA's future contributed greatly to this happy development. I am grateful for this and to the faculty, students, and graduates whose devoted efforts made it possible. I earnestly hope that SUA will continue to strive for still greater heights and thus live up to all of your expectations.

In 2010, Soka University of Japan introduced its new Global Citizenship Program. Founded on our established tradition of humanistic education, this unique program will further energize our cultivation of the world citizens required in this age of globalization. Our intention is to foster the kind of cultivated, creative individuals you have described. New students in all departments can apply to participate in the program. While doing the academic work required by their department and thoroughly mastering the basic curriculum common to all areas of study, they can strive to cultivate spirit, skills, and service experience.[8]

I hope that, while facing many challenges, they will strengthen the current of humanistic education, which is opening twenty-first-century horizons of peace and harmonious coexistence. I intend to devote myself even more energetically to helping them achieve this aim. People trained according to Soka educational practices are continuing to pursue the path of this mission.

The Solidest Thing

IKEDA: The bonds of friendship are the most beautiful, strongest, and most precious things in life. Many examples can be cited from world history, like the shining, celebrated friendships of Johann Wolfgang Goethe and Friedrich Schiller, and of the early nineteenth-century English poet William Wordsworth and English poet, critic, and philosopher Samuel Taylor Coleridge. I have memories of such friendships in my own youth.

Though Wordsworth and Coleridge suffered severe setbacks in their sensitive younger years, they developed through their struggles a friendship that gave them fresh hope in life. They published the collection *Lyrical Ballads* together. The product of their mutual inspiration—despite the fact that they were temperamentally and stylistically worlds apart—*Lyrical Ballads* became a work of monumental significance to the Romantic Movement.

Wordsworth later dedicated *The Prelude* to his peerless friend, Coleridge. This long poem of more than eight thousand lines, based on autobiographical reflections, is a kind of symphonic suite with an appeal to his friend as its main theme.

Thou, O honored Friend!
Who in my thoughts art ever at my side,
Uphold, as heretofore, my fainting steps.[1]

Each stanza shines in testimony to the friendship between Wordsworth and Coleridge.

WIDER: Wordsworth recognized the doubled strength in friendship: the support directly given by friend to friend as well as the equally important strength created by shared knowledge.

The nineteenth century has given us some of the most powerful and complex friendships—the friendships within the women's rights movement in the United States, the philosophical and literary friendships that were equally centered in social reform, the Transcendentalist circle of friends. As Emerson asked, "Should not the society of my friend be to me poetic, pure, universal, and great as nature itself?"[2]

Important to every generation and in every era, friendship has never been more important than it is today. While I see a great hunger for friendship, I also see an equal fear for its existence. Contemporary society increasingly reduces friendship to no more than another dimension of self-interest. "Friends" are used as a means for self-advancement, and friendship is irrevocably compromised. In our current age, where every hour—indeed, minute—is accounted for, the unconfined and unconfinable nature of friendship asks us to follow a different path.

IKEDA: For this reason, we need to know what is true friendship. Emerson believed that it results only from the unstinting application of time and effort. Familiarity with their works made him long to meet Wordsworth and Coleridge so strongly that finally he decided to travel to Europe. He remembered encounters like this with people better than he did the most beautiful scenery or famous historical sites.

He wrote, "When they [friendships] are real, they are not glass thread or frostwork, but the solidest thing we know."[3] The older I grow, the more deeply I agree with this statement. This is why I always encourage the students of the Soka Junior and Senior High Schools and of Soka University to use the precious springtime of youth to form bonds that will be an encouragement throughout life, no matter what happens.

WIDER: I, too, encourage my students to form vigorous and truthful friendships. In his essay "Friendship," Emerson names truth and tenderness as key elements. Friends must be absolutely truthful with one another, even to the point of discomfort. What you say to your friend may not be enjoyable to hear, but your respect for both the truth and for your friend demands plain and honest language.

At the same time, you must respect the power in truthfulness and never abuse it by using words to lord over your friend. Emerson's tenderness never covers the truth but reveals it without malice or manipulation. I might use the word *empathy* here. Delivering truth requires reciprocity: the ability to think apart from oneself, to consider others, and to see, as best one can, through another's eyes.

IKEDA: Romain Rolland related how he formed a lasting friendship in his school days, a story I once shared with students of the Soka Junior and Senior High Schools. At the École Normale Supérieure (Normal High School), on the day when rooms and roommates were being assigned, no one wanted to room with a late-coming student named André Suarès, who was later active as a writer.[4] Some were jealous of the reputation for excellence that preceded him or were prejudiced against him as a Jew. But Rolland welcomed him as a roommate.

Other students criticized and shunned Rolland. He took no notice, treated Suarès with kindness, and became his friend. When schoolmates tried to have Suarès expelled on trumped-up charges, Rolland strongly opposed and honorably exposed their plot. The two became fast friends for life.

I refer to this story when encouraging young people to form enduring friendships. Indeed friendship is one of life's greatest treasures. In today's information society, deep communication between individuals is in ever greater demand.

WIDER: With means of communication like the Internet, it is easy to hold conversations anytime and anywhere. And yet I often wonder and think aloud with my students about how technology changes our ability to converse face to face. In offices, there is the strange situation of emailing somebody just a couple doors away. Before the Internet, you would just walk down the hall and talk with the person. We joke about people who text each other when they're in the same room. I walk across campus and as likely see students talking into their phones as to the people around them. It seems that people feel more comfortable dealing with others via a screen or a machine.

While there is a place for the sense of immediacy provided by the electronic devices we use, there is also a real danger of not giving deep and full attention to any one person or situation. Everyone seems to be talking at once, and in all this clamor of commentary, no one may be listening. A person's attention dissipates. The "conversation" settles into a repetition of clichés and remarks that veneer a brittle surface.

As I look around me, so many seem to be on "overload," with too much to do, too many pieces of equipment demanding their response, and a strained sense that the "put-together image" they present is just about to crack. No wonder insecurity develops, and individuals feel even more alone.

Of course, there are things I truly value in the Internet. For example, it can connect people across distances. I have so enjoyed conversing with members of the women's and young women's divisions in Japan and with Soka students, keeping up on their projects. In Wordsworth's sense, this is one power of friendship: "who in my thoughts art ever at my side."[5]

All the more so when we send thoughts to be with our friends when we physically can't. This seems an extension of the vital connection between human beings that Emerson, Thoreau, and Fuller wrote about so forcefully. Friendship becomes the home for such vitality, but the inhabitants need to leave their self-interested minds at the door and be ready to attend to the real and difficult challenges asked by true relations.

IKEDA: I also want to remind young people of this by borrowing these words from Emerson: "Let him not intermeddle with this [friendship]. Leave to the diamond its ages to grow, nor expect to accelerate the births of the eternal."[6]

TRAVELING THE ROAD TOGETHER

WIDER: What powerful remembrances of friendships do you preserve?

IKEDA: I have made many lasting friendships over my past fifty years promoting peace, culture, and education throughout the world. For instance, I shall always remember Rem Khokhlov, rector of Moscow State University, whom I met on my first visit to the Soviet Union. It was during the Cold War, when relations between his country and mine were frozen in suspicion and hostility. It seemed that the deep-rooted mistrust and animosity would never thaw.

Although the Soviet Union was a communist state, I knew those living there were human beings just like us. In addition, the Soviet Union was a neighbor to Japan. I was convinced that we could somehow foster mutual understanding.

Then Moscow State University invited me, as Soka University founder, to visit. In spite of an outcry in Japan, I made up my mind to go. I wanted to ignite even a single light of friendship, to sow even a handful of seeds of friendship.

At the Moscow airport on September 8, 1974, a calmly smiling Rector Khokhlov headed the welcoming party. I was forty-six at the time, and Rector Khokhlov, a radiation physicist, was forty-eight. As we shook hands, I began explaining my educational convictions. With shining eyes, he firmly returned the pressure of my grip. Good faith and sincerity were evident in everything he said; I felt certain he was a real seeker of the path to friendship.

WIDER: In that very year, Aleksandr Solzhenitsyn was exiled for publishing his novel *The Gulag Archipelago*, which was critical of the Soviet system. It was bold of you to visit the Soviet Union at a time when tensions ran high.

IKEDA: Actually, when we deplaned, both parties looked tense and insecure, but they gradually relaxed after a few minutes watching Rector Khokhlov and me chatting amiably. That evening, Rector Khokhlov gave us a welcome dinner in the restaurant of our lodgings. I delivered greetings, saying that building bridges of friendship requires us to look a hundred or two hundred years into the future and open the way for future generations. I went on to say that this was my reason for affording maximum emphasis to educational exchanges, which give birth to long-lasting exchanges free of political or economic domination. And I added my conviction that, connecting not only Japan and the Soviet Union but also the countries of the world, such friendly exchanges can bring the whole world together, promoting a rising tide of global peace.

Thereafter our discussion grew so enthusiastic and protracted that, before we knew it, our ice cream had melted. I remember everyone laughing heartily at my joke: The warmth of our friendship had melted the ice cream, creating a new Soviet drink.

The next day, I visited the magnificent campus of Moscow State University. This was the start of exchanges between Soka University and Moscow State University. Rector Khokhlov and I engaged in frank exchanges on a variety of subjects, including peace, culture, and education. My meeting with him was more than enough to justify my visit, I felt.

Throughout our stay there, he took excellent care of us. He and his wife, Elena, saw us off at the airport. I thanked him for the unforgettable kindness he had shown us and invited the two of them to visit Soka University and the Soka Junior and Senior High Schools. He responded with a vigorous nod of assent, and they did so only six weeks later.

When I visited the Soviet Union a second time, in May 1975, Moscow State University held several commemorative events to welcome me. And in April 1977, Rector Khokhlov made a return visit to Japan, during which he tried to obtain some over-the-counter medicine for his mother, recuperating from an illness. Learning that he was unable to get what he needed, I took immediate steps to have the medication delivered.

But that summer, I received the shocking news that he had been killed in a mountain-climbing accident. I was struck dumb by this unbelievable tragedy. I learned that, in spite of his own worsening physical condition, he had sent his young companions down the mountain to safety. This is exactly how I would have expected him to behave.

When I visited the Soviet Union in May 1981, I prayed for his repose at his grave. I also paid a visit to his home on the grounds of Moscow State University, where I spoke with Elena and his two sons, students at the time.

WIDER: You formed a profound association with him.

IKEDA: Approximately thirty years have passed. His older son, Alexei R. Khokhlov, is now vice-rector of Moscow State University, and his younger son, Dmitry R. Khokhlov, is a professor there.

Rector Khokhlov once suggested that we continue our discussions and travel a spiritual Silk Road together. In the spirit of his request, I conducted a dialogue with Anatoli A. Logunov, who succeeded Mr. Khokhlov as rector of Moscow State University in 1977. Our dialogue was later published in two books, *Daisan no niji no hashi* (The Third Rainbow Bridge) and *Kagaku to shukyo* (Science and Religion). In addition, I have published two dialogues[7] with Victor A. Sadovnichy, current rector of Moscow State University. Our dialogues are still in progress.

Since the conclusion of an agreement on educational cooperation between Soka University and Moscow State University in 1975, we have sent 300 students and faculty members there; more than 600 Russian students from Moscow State University and other Russian institutions, including the Russian Far Eastern University, have come to Soka University. Training scholars, educators, and interpreters, these institutions take the lead in cultivating amicable relations between our two nations.

The friendship that Rector Khokhlov and I established more than thirty years ago became a line of connecting points that are now coalescing to form an expansive space. I am determined to devote even greater effort to fulfilling his wish to extend the Silk Road of the spirit.

WIDER: Your many years of work for amity between Russia and Japan beautifully illustrate the promise and power of friendship. Indeed, as your friendship with Rector Khokhlov shows, peace grows through this dedication to connecting with others and providing opportunities to share thought, creativity, and open questions. As many have said, peace is not war's weak opposite; it is its own complex and challenging condition.

No one speaks better to the presence and nature of peace than Elise Boulding, the longtime peace scholar and activist who passed away in the summer of 2010. In a world plagued by war, she set forth a most powerful idea, one that can indeed be taken readily into daily practice. She talked and wrote about creating islands of peace cultures—places that "promote peaceable diversity" and "deal creatively with the conflicts and differences that appear in every society, because no two humans are alike."[8]

Understanding the connections between peace and diversity is key. As Emerson said, "All are needed by each one; / Nothing is fair or good alone."[9]

So, too, is creativity fundamental. The current predominant ways of addressing difference and conflict are signally lacking in creativity. Boulding went on to depict how a society's institutions must reflect the hard but satisfying work of peace: creating "institutionalized arrangements that promote mutual caring, well-being, and the equitable sharing of the earth's resources among its members and with all living beings."[10]

This seems very much like your own work of erecting bridges of friendship, so that individuals from different backgrounds can come together. Nations may then follow where their citizens can truly lead.

IKEDA: Dr. Elise Boulding was one of the great pioneers who opened new horizons in peace studies. Placing unbounded hope in our movement for peace culture, she participated in the supervision of some SGI exhibitions, including "Women and the Culture of Peace."

I recall that we discussed the idea of "islands of peace culture" in *Into Full Flower: Making Peace Cultures Happen,* the dialogue she and I published (2010). It originated from a conviction of her husband, Dr. Kenneth Boulding, who often said that the culture of peace is no more than a small island in the war-culture ocean. But as long as one such island exists, he said, it is sure to multiply into two, then three. I recall how strongly she emphasized transmitting this ideal of her husband to the next generation.

Dr. Boulding, about one and a half months before her passing, talked with Virginia Benson, former director of the Ikeda Center for Peace, Learning, and Dialogue, and told her cheerfully:

> Peace cultures don't just happen. We together have to make them happen. We have to start where we are. The thing about peace being born is that, just as the sun has to rise, peace also rises every day.

Furthermore, she urged: "Don't stop. Enjoy what you are doing. Peace is about being and doing. It's the happiest thing in the world you can do."

As Dr. Boulding continually told us so enthusiastically until her last day, the creation of peace should be our eternal challenge. In the process of creating peace through heart-to-heart connections and the bond of friendship, we can find true satisfaction and joy in life. It is my renewed determination and sincere hope to bravely advance along the royal road for peace together with you and other valuable friends of the world.

Infinite Power Inside

IKEDA: Whitman was, again, a poet of the people, with a great love for the people (see Conversation Twelve). He had a deep understanding of their greatness and sang the praises of their lives.

In his later years, he expressed his pride in being one of the people:

> I see how lucky I was that I was myself thrown out early upon the average earth—to wrestle for myself—among the masses of people—never living in coteries: that I have always lived cheek by jowl with the common people—yes indeed, not only bred that way but born that way.[1]

Born to a family that produced nori (edible seaweed), I, too, consider it the greatest pride of my life that I have always lived with the common people and struggled for their sake. Nothing can compare to the people's greatness. Anything divorced from the solid ground of the people is no more than a castle in the air.

WIDER: Your poetry and other writings send the powerful message that peace will be built by the hands of the people. It cannot be left to the leaders.

I am reminded of Emerson's ideas about heroism. Though a good friend of Thomas Carlyle, Emerson strongly disagreed with his ideas about heroes. Carlyle followed the "great man" notion, focusing on the supposedly special individuals who stood out from and above the rest of society. Emerson, on the other hand, suggested a much different understanding, pointedly seen in his book title *Representative Men*. The "great" weren't apart from us: They were, in fact, part of us. Their specific power or particular deeds represented different aspects of humanity. Their qualities and capabilities were fundamentally ours as well. The emphasis is yet again on potential and its fact within every human being.

As Emerson said in "The Method of Nature": "A man should know himself for a necessary actor. A link was wanting between two craving parts of nature, and he was hurled into being as the bridge over that yawning need."[2] Each person could do something that no one else could, and that something was essential to the well being of the world. We could not hide behind "larger than life" heroes. In fact, Emerson worried that such adulation provided a sorry escape route for individuals who might then rationalize their own passivity as diligent followers to another's demanding leadership.

It also opened the danger of abused power, encouraging self-aggrandizement on the part of the "hero." Always cautious of hierarchies, Emerson reminded his audiences that each person carried the potential for greatness. The ordinary is no barrier but in fact the very place where change must be deeply rooted.

IKEDA: Emerson boldly proclaimed: "As to what we call the masses, and common men; there are no common men. All men are at last of a size."[3] He also wrote, "The fairest fortune that can befall man, is to be guided by his daemon to that which is truly his own."[4]

I especially urge young people, on whom the future depends, to heed these words. No matter what the present situation, the important thing is to hold onto one's dreams and hopes while facing whatever challenges arise day to day. There is absolutely no need to succumb to a sense of inferiority and insignificance. Each of us must move forward, confident that there is a mission in this world that we alone can fulfill.

President Toda said:

> It is especially important to believe in yourself when you are young. But that's often hard to do—especially for the young, who are frequently emotional and confused. The more self-confident young people are, the less likely they are to be defeated. They must have something of their own to believe in; they must believe in themselves.

WIDER: The strength that arises from within is a matter of deepest importance. Whether today or in years past, education rarely addresses this strength. It's left to its own devices, easily distorted, or set adrift.

Emerson's thoughts on education speak directly to this absent essential. In "The Divinity School Address," he sums up the teacher-student relationship: "Truly speaking, it is not instruction, but provocation, that I can receive from another soul."[5] He doesn't mean *provocation* in the reactive sense of irritation but rather as vital stimulation. No passive recipient, the student is actively and urgently encouraged to think without bounds and without predetermined answers.

IKEDA: Emerson also wrote, "Man is endogenous, and education is his unfolding."[6] This is his keen insight. In other words, good education provides the stimulus for the growth of our inner potential.

THE NATURAL COLLEGE

WIDER: True education should provoke us to say: "Oh, what does this mean? What are the implications?" or "I've never thought of it that way, and now that I begin to see differently, what happens when I take this idea further?"

Emerson's ideas came into American education in multiple ways—through Elizabeth Palmer Peabody and her kindergarten movement, through Jane Addams and her settlement houses—but best known is the powerful reform of American education undertaken by John Dewey in the first part of the twentieth century.

IKEDA: President Makiguchi was also drawn to Dewey's ideas on educational reform. In our discussion of Dewey's philosophy,[7] Professor Larry Hickman, past president of the John Dewey Society, pointed out something important in connection with modern education: In many educational environments today, students are taught to be value extractors but not value creators. True happiness, however, consists in enriching the meanings of our lives. This, according to Professor Hickman, is the core of Dewey's pedagogic philosophy. It is an idea that resonates deeply with our Soka educational ideals.

WIDER: As Professor Hickman so aptly comments, extraction and consumption dominate education at this moment. The United States all too rarely practices a Deweyean model, in which education works as a creative means for developing human potential. An active reader of Emerson's works, Dewey distrusted rote learning and emphasized individual and free inquiry.

Today, Emerson's idea of provocation has been swallowed up in standardization. In the current climate, "successful" students are those who willingly perform to task. They are pleased to excel if you tell them what to do. They either suppress their many questions or learn to take satisfaction in the questions that earn them rewards. Other students manage, turn on the autopilot of their minds, or turn off their inquiring impulses altogether. No wonder American youth are either charged with apathy or mimicry: They have been given so little opportunity to feel and respond to Emerson's healthy "provocation" to thought.

IKEDA: Intellectual stimulation, or provocation, should be the purpose of a good education. This method of teaching was employed in ancient times by such figures as Socrates of Greece, Shakyamuni of India, and Confucius of China, all of whom engaged in daily dialogue with their students.

Emerson made these thought-provoking comments on dialogue:

> Happy the natural college thus self-instituted around every
> natural teacher; the young men of Athens around Socrates;
> of Alexandria around Plotinus; of Paris around Abelard; of
> Germany around Fichte, or Niebuhr, or Goethe: in short
> the natural sphere of every leading mind.[8]

Such examples of mutual inspiration illuminated their ages with the light of hope.

As I already explained, I received private instruction under my mentor for ten years (see Conversation Twelve). For me, this Toda University was not only an opportunity to acquire knowledge in a wide variety of fields but—through dialogue with my mentor—to forge my character and develop and uplift myself. Each lecture was a real struggle for me, and I was not allowed to take notes. I couldn't allow myself to miss a single word of my teacher's lectures. Everything that I am today I owe to him.

WIDER: Would that more people took learning as seriously as do the students in the "natural college." In conventional education, students often talk casually about how many answers they can afford to miss and still get a good grade. Here you talk about not missing a word. Everything matters. Your experience of learning with Mr. Toda clearly proved to be an invaluable part of a true education.

I contrast this with the memory work often enforced in school. Many of us have indeed felt shipwrecked by the kind of memorization demanded of us.

A particular discussion in class comes to mind. We were talking about how different "rote memorization" is from "knowing by heart." One student shared her experience as an exchange student in Russia. Thinking to create a place of connection, her Russian host family asked what American poems she could share with them. Given their own longstanding tradition of learning poems by heart, they assumed the same for her. But she had memorized for school assignments in a way that only engaged the surface of her mind.

Ask any of my students, and they will lament how they can memorize for a test and then lose that information in a few days time. But what they have learned by heart stays with them. It becomes a living memory. It matters so much that you cannot forget.

And like a pebble dropped into a still pond, circles expand from the simple center. Not only do you remember, you know how to care for this memory. You cannot forget your ongoing responsibility to what you have learned, to the experience behind this learning, and to those who also need to know what lives so powerfully in and through mind and heart.

What is memorized fades; what is known by heart endures. And yet we rarely encourage students to take their school work to heart, instead emphasizing a cool and so-called objective distance between themselves and their work. We often fail to provide opportunities where knowledge can be truly absorbed and internalized.

IKEDA: President Makiguchi also advocated for the true internalization of knowledge. He held that the practice of evaluating children's personalities on the basis of how much classroom material they could memorize was erroneous and destructive:

> It is not enough to recognize and memorize the verbal formulas that express truths; the true duty of the teacher is to show his pupils how to apply those truths to life, increasing the power to create the values of good, gain, and beauty.[9]

In other words, education does not end with acquiring knowledge but must lead to a life that employs what is learned to maximize creativity and makes use of learning to benefit others and society as a whole.

President Makiguchi, though recognizing the great diversity in how we live, categorized people generally into three types: (1) Those who, while fearful of the powerful, are arrogant toward anyone weaker than themselves. Such people get ahead in the world by cheating others and by self-deception; (2) The self-satisfied who, while honest themselves, avoid matters unrelated to themselves and neither dislike the evil nor feel especially close to the good; and (3) Those who, unsatisfied with only their own happiness, always share the joys and sorrows of others and, understanding things correctly, work for the sake of justice, unafraid of opponents. He insisted that educators should admonish against the first two ways of living and encourage the third.

No matter how much knowledge one acquires or how powerful one's mental abilities are, they are meaningless without a solid conviction and philosophy of life, without the sense of responsibility you refer to.

HOPE

WIDER: I turn particularly to Mr. Makiguchi's emphasis that our individual happiness is never an end in itself. I am greatly concerned about the current heightened individualism and attention to self-gain. When individualism is put in the service of materialism, we distort the human being into a small-minded thinker who values acquisition over relation and self-selection over integral connection.

As Emerson said:

> A man is a little thing whilst he works by and for himself, but, when he gives voice to the rules of love and justice, is godlike, his word is current in all countries; and all men, though his enemies, are made his friends.[10]

In service to—or you might say addicted to—acquisition, we have developed a soul-deadening efficiency. Rather than asking how something might be done in a way that is most just for all, we fall into a short-sighted utilitarianism that values how quick and how much over how lasting and for whom. We fail to cultivate deep-rooted connections with others, especially those with whom we differ. We seal ourselves off in a superficially connected world, on our cell phones, our mp3 players, with our headphones, attached to our screens, barely attending to the sound of a simple, direct human voice.

Of course, this situation can't be changed overnight. Technology is an opened Pandora's Box, and yet, the mind is a wonderful place. We need not become the tools of our machines. As Emerson noted, every individual remains an active player in his or her own life, no matter how imprisoning the circumstances.

Emerson would never give up on the potential innate within each person. This trust formed the basis of his understanding of how reform could truly be accomplished. Until individuals themselves changed, any imposed change would remain tentative, awaiting the true and lasting change of heart.

IKEDA: The human revolution movement of the SGI, too, promotes the activation and manifestation of the inherent goodness within each person, spreading waves of spiritual revolution throughout society to build a better world—always through the religious practice of each individual. It is a consciousness-raising movement to expand humanistic education through the people's efforts.

Buddhism teaches the infinite power inherent equally in each individual human life from a variety of perspectives. Like a flame reaching up toward the heavens, life has the power to convert suffering into energy for value creation and to illuminate the darkness of this world; like a wind blowing in all directions without obstruction, life can carry away all hardship and adversity; like a cool, clear stream, it has the power to purify all the impurities of this world; and like the earth nurturing all plants and trees, it has the power to protect all people impartially and treat them with equal compassion.

The core of our human revolution movement is drawing out, in both ourselves and others, this fundamental power of life that resides deep within all people, making it shine its brightest.

WIDER: Hearing your words about the human revolution movement, I cannot stop thinking of Emerson's emphasis on the creative force available to all.

It is sad that religion today is often the greatest divisive force among human beings. As did Emerson in the 1840s, I call for renewed attention to the affinities across cultures, times, and places.

Certainly Buddhism's emphasis on our profound and deeply rooted interconnectedness gives me great hope, as does its emphasis on sustained listening. Buddhism thus encourages the boundless potential of the individual in light of our responsibility to others. I turn again to the word *hope*—the strong-hearted hope rooted in the full range of daily life.

For all the readers who have joined us on this journey, I celebrate their participation and look forward to working together with them so that true relations beat as the heart of our world. This dialogue's true "end" is endless. While our musings will no longer be structured in the same way, our shared thoughts and commitment to peace through friendship go forth, truly speaking in our lives. I stand with a thankful heart for all this dialogue has opened to me and, I trust, to others. With my mother, I say, "A grateful heart is a happy heart."

Emerson called us to stand in true relation to one another: The twenty-first century faces no greater challenge.

IKEDA: This is indeed a guideline for the new age. Our discussion has enabled me to study and come to understand in greater depth the philosophical core of the American Renaissance, which extolled the dignity of life and strove for its great flowering, for building a society of peace and harmonious coexistence.

I hope that, together with you, I can work for the realization of a global renaissance in the twenty-first century. Let me round out our dialogue by expressing my profound gratitude to you and by quoting some of my favorite Emerson verses:

> O friend, my bosom said,
> Through thee alone the sky is arched,

Through thee the rose is red,
All things through thee take nobler form,
And look beyond the earth,
And is the mill-round of our fate
A sun-path in thy worth.
Me too thy nobleness has taught
To master my despair;
The fountains of my hidden life
Are through thy friendship fair.[11]

WIDER: I, too, cherish these words from Emerson and will treasure them all the more deeply and fully through your singing them here as we conclude this part of our always ongoing dialogue. Emerson speaks so beautifully and so truly about the transformative power of friendship. There is no abstraction here. He is particular and present—person to person, friend to friend.

The "mill-round of our fate" becomes a "sun-path." Despair is no longer our master. Our best potential, though at some points it may be hidden, emerges "through thy friendship fair." I think he means "fair" in both senses of our English word: beautiful and just.

As Whitman might have, I celebrate the friendship we share, transformative in my own life and I trust for all whom I daily meet in the spirit of true and profound friendship. The strong and life-lifting words of Shakyamuni Buddha resound: "Friendship is everything." I indeed look forward to working with you in the twenty-first century for a global renaissance that brings forth the resounding music of peace-creating cultures through expansive and generous collaboration.

Notes

PREFACE BY DAISAKU IKEDA

1. Paraphrased from Ralph Waldo Emerson, "The Poet" in *Essays and Lectures*, Joel Porte, ed. (New York: The Library of America, 1983) pp. 459–60: "The poet knows that he speaks adequately, then only when he speaks somewhat wildly, or, 'with the flower of the mind;' not with the intellect, used as an organ, but with the intellect released from all service, and suffered to take its direction from its celestial life; or, as the ancients were wont to express themselves, not with intellect alone, but with the intellect inebriated by nectar."

2. On July 3, 1945, Josei Toda was released from Toyotama Prison after being incarcerated for two years. On July 3, 1957, Daisaku Ikeda was arrested on trumped-up charges of violating election laws. He was eventually cleared of any wrongdoing. July 3 is commemorated today by SGI members worldwide as the Day of Mentor and Disciple.

3. Arnold J. Toynbee, *Experiences* (New York and London: Oxford University Press, 1969), pp. 320–21.

4. This magnitude 9.0 undersea earthquake, often referred to in Japan as the Great East Japan Earthquake, struck about 43 miles off Japan's eastern coast on Friday, March 11, 2011. It was the strongest earthquake known to have hit Japan, and the fifth most powerful in the world (since modern recordkeeping began in 1900). The earthquake triggered powerful tsunami waves as high as 130 feet, which travelled inland up to six miles in Japan's Tohoku and Sendai areas. There were

reported to be 15,883 deaths and 2,667 missing throughout twenty-two prefectures affected.

CONVERSATION ONE
NEW ADVENTURES

1. Emerson, *Nature* in *Essays and Lectures*, p. 48.
2. Soka schools: The Soka Junior and Senior High Schools—established by Daisaku Ikeda in Kodaira, Tokyo, in 1968—were the beginning of the Soka school system, which today includes kindergartens, elementary, junior, and senior high schools, a university in Tokyo, and a university in Aliso Viejo, Calif. Kindergartens have also been established in Hong Kong, Singapore, Malaysia, South Korea, and Brazil. The schools are based on Soka education.
3. Emerson, "Circles" in *Essays and Lectures*, p. 414.
4. Daisaku Ikeda, "A Symphony of Great and Noble Mothers—Dedicated to the Gentle, Wise, and Courageous Mothers of Kosen-rufu," March 30, 2012, *World Tribune*, p. 7.
5. Nichiren, *The Writings of Nichiren Daishonin*, vol. I (Tokyo: Soka Gakkai, 1999), p. 955.
6. Soka education: The educational system based on the pedagogy of founding Soka Gakkai president and educator Tsunesaburo Makiguchi, who believed that the focus of education should be the lifelong happiness of the learner. Makiguchi was concerned with the development of the unique personality of each child, and he emphasized the importance of leading a socially contributive life. *See* Daisaku Ikeda, *Soka Education: For the Happiness of the Individual* (Santa Monica, Calif.: Middleway Press, 2010).
7. The other four are: "Do not cause trouble to others, and always take responsibility for your own actions," "Be considerate and polite, reject violence, and value trustworthiness and cooperation," "Boldly speak out for your beliefs and act courageously for the sake of truth and justice," and "Cultivate an enterprising spirit and become respectable leaders of Japan and the world."
8. The Toda Institute for Global Peace and Policy Research held its conference, themed "The Power of Dialogue in a Time of Global Crisis," on November 22–23, 2009. The purpose of the conference was to find the role and power of dialogue in conflict transformation, peace

building, and sustainable development. Dr. Wider gave the keynote address, titled "Peace Through Listening: Conversations Across Time and Place."

9. Emerson, "Circles" in *Essays and Lectures*, p. 379.

10. Daisaku Ikeda, "Scaling Life's Mountains," Nov. 22, 2002, *World Tribune*, p. 1.

11. Daisaku Ikeda, *The Poet's Star* (Tokyo: Soka Gakkai, 2003), p. 147.

12. Walt Whitman, *Leaves of Grass* in *Poetry and Prose*, Justin Kaplan, ed. (New York: Library of America, 1996), p. 611. (*Leaves of Grass* was published anonymously in 1855. Whitman revised it nine times before publishing the version cited here, often referred to as his "deathbed" edition, in 1891–92. This quote does not appear in his early editions.)

Conversation Two
University of All Knowledges

1. The Haudenosaunee ("People of the Longhouse" or, more accurately, "They Are Building a Long House"), also known as the Iroquois (French) or Six Nations (English), formed a league that includes the Mohawk, Oneida, Onondaga, Cayuga, Seneca, and Tuscarora nations. When Europeans first arrived in North America, the Haudenosaunee were centered in what is now the northeastern United States. Today the Haudenosaunee live primarily in New York, Quebec, and Ontario. *See* Bruce Elliott Johansen, Barbara Alice Mann, eds., *Encyclopedia of the Haudenosaunee* (Westport, Conn.: Greenwood Publishing Company, 2000).

2. Nichiren, *The Writings*, vol. I, p. 279.

3. *See* Elise Boulding and Daisaku Ikeda, *Into Full Flower: Making Peace Cultures Happen* (Cambridge, Mass.: Dialogue Path Press, 2010), p. 61.

4. Emerson, *Nature* in *Essays and Lectures*, p. 10.

5. Ibid., p. 23.

6. Ralph Waldo Emerson, "Science" in *The Early Lectures of Ralph Waldo Emerson*, vol. 1, Stephen E. Whicher and Robert E. Spiller, eds. (New York: Harvard University Press, 1959), p. 73.

7. In his lecture "The Individual," Emerson stated: "The fact that the Individual mind is a university of all knowledges wherein all particular

natures find their representative idea, each new experience discloses and confirms. All men are of one essence.… So does the individual mind read universal history in a few persons; in one person." *See* Ralph Waldo Emerson, *The Early Lectures of Ralph Waldo Emerson*, vol. 2, Stephen E. Whicher, Robert E. Spiller, and Wallace E. Williams, eds. (Cambridge, Mass.: Harvard University Press, 1964), p. 178.

8. Ralph Walso Emerson, "Country Life" in *The Later Lectures of Ralph Waldo Emerson, 1845–1871*, vol. 2, Ronald A. Bosco and Joel Myerson, eds. (Athens, Ga.: University of Georgia Press, 2010), p. 63.

CONVERSATION THREE
THE ENCOURAGING VOICE

1. This dialogue was originally published serially in Japanese in *Pumpkin*, a Japanese magazine for women readers, November 2009–February 2011.

2. Mohandas K. Gandhi, *The Wit and Wisdom of Gandhi*, Homer A. Jack, ed. (New York: Courier Dover Publications, 2012), p. 144.

3. Ralph Waldo Emerson, "Education" in *The Collected Works of Ralph Waldo Emerson*, vol. 10: *Lectures and Biographical Sketches*, Edward Waldo Emerson, ed. (Boston and New York: Houghton, Mifflin and Company, 1903–1904), p. 143.

4. As related by singer-songwriter John McCutcheon in the song "Sydney/Joe Hill" on his 2009 album *Untold*.

5. Daisaku Ikeda, *Discussions on Youth* (Santa Monica, Calif.: World Tribune Press, 2012), p. 76.

6. Ibid., p. 77.

7. Personal communication.

8. In the April 1970 issue of *Gramophone*, interviewer Alan Blythe wrote: "His father had the young Eugene playing the violin when he was just two and at five he entered the Budapest Royal Academy of Music. Ormandy said he had no real childhood as others experienced it but one day he did go out to play soccer in secret—only living to rue the day. Five other hefty youngsters sat on him so heavily that the little boy's hip was broken, an injury that bothers him to this day." *See* <http://www.gramophone.co.uk/features/focus/90th-anniversary-interviews-eugene-ormandy>.

9. John Andrew Frey, *A Victor Hugo Encyclopedia* (Westport, Conn.: Greenwood Press, 1999), pp. 197–98. "Once a week on Guernsey, he offered a splendid meal to the poor children of the island."

10. Mary Moody Emerson was Ralph Waldo Emerson's aunt and first significant teacher. The Reverend William Emerson—Mary's older brother and Ralph Waldo Emerson's father—died when Ralph Waldo was eight. Mary moved into the family home to help care for the six children.

11. *See* John Ingulsrud, Kate Allen, *Reading Japan Cool: Patterns of Manga Literacy* (Lanham, Md.: Lexington Books, 2010), p. 30.

12. *See* Robert D. Richardson, *Emerson: The Mind on Fire* (Berkeley, Calif.: University of California Press, 1995), pp. 21–22.

13. Edward Waldo Emerson, *Emerson in Concord—A Memoir: Written for the "Social Circle" in Concord, Massachusetts* (Boston and New York: Houghton, Mifflin and Company, 1889), p. 21.

14. James Elliot Cabot, *A Memoir of Ralph Waldo Emerson* (Boston and New York: Houghton, Mifflin and Company, 1888), p. 35.

15. For example, Emerson wrote, "To stand in true relations with men in a false age is worth a fit of insanity, is it not?" *See* Emerson, "Friendship" in *Essays and Lectures*, p. 347.

16. Nichiren, *The Writings*, vol. I, p. 851.

17. Nichiren, *The Record of the Orally Transmitted Teachings*, Burton Watson, trans. (Tokyo: Soka Gakkai, 2004), p. 146.

18. Ibid.

CONVERSATION FOUR
ALL THINGS CONNECTED

1. Nichiren, *The Writings*, vol. I, p. 94.

2. Emerson, *Nature* in *Essays and Lectures*, p. 11.

3. Burton Watson, trans., *The Lotus Sutra and Its Opening and Closing Sutras* (Tokyo: Soka Gakkai, 2009), p. 365. It reads, "If you see a person who accepts and upholds this sutra, you should rise and greet him from afar, showing him the same respect you would a buddha."

4. Personal communication.

5. Perestroika ("restructuring"): The policy of restructuring and reforming the economic, political, and social systems of the U.S.S.R. promoted, beginning in 1985, by Mikhail Gorbachev.

CONVERSATION FIVE
SUBLIME MOTIVATIONS

1. The documentary *Louisa May Alcott: The Woman Behind 'Little Women'* aired in 2009 on PBS stations throughout the United States and won several awards, including Booklist Best Video of the Year.

2. The name "Minutemen" refers to the soldiers' ability to spring into action at a minute's notice. They were mostly farmers or craftsmen; however, in times of emergency they would immediately gather together to handle the situation.

3. Alcott's *Little Women*, written at Orchard House, was originally published in two volumes: *Little Women* (1868) and *Good Wives* (1869). Starting in 1880, both were published as one book, titled *Little Women*. Two sequels followed: *Little Men* (1871) and *Jo's Boys* (1886).

4. Ednah D. Cheny, ed., *Louisa May Alcott: Her Life, Letters and Journals* (Boston: Roberts Brothers, 1890), p. 127.

5. Ralph Waldo Emerson, "Address at the Opening of Concord Free Public Library" in *The Complete Works of Ralph Waldo Emerson*, vol. 11: *Miscellanies* (Boston and New York: Houghton, Mifflin and Company, 1903–1904), p. 503.

6. Emerson, "Experience" in *Essays and Lectures*, p. 492.

7. Nancy Newhall, ed., *Time in New England* (New York: Oxford University Press, 1950), p. 113.

8. See Phyllis Cole, *Mary Moody Emerson and the Origins of Transcendentalism: A Family History* (New York: Oxford University Press, 2002).

9. See Nancy Simmons, ed., *Selected Letters of Mary Moody Emerson* (Atlanta, Ga.: University of Georgia Press, 1993).

10. "Little-endians" is an allusion to the orthodox Lilliputians in Jonathan Swift's work *Gulliver's Travels*. Little-endians insist that hardboiled eggs must be eaten starting with the little end.

11. Ralph Waldo Emerson, *The Journals and Miscellaneous Notebooks of Ralph Waldo Emerson*, vol. 4, William H. Gilman, Ralph H. Orth, et al., eds. (Cambridge, Mass., and London: Harvard University Press, 1960–1982), p. 353.

12. Arnold Toynbee, *Civilization on Trial* (New York: Oxford University Press, 1948), p. 213.

13. Ralph Waldo Emerson, "Address at a Women's Rights Convention, 20 September, 1855" in *The Selected Lectures of Ralph Waldo Emerson*,

Ronald A. Bosco and Joel Myerson, eds. (Athens, Ga.: University of Georgia Press, 2005), p. 216.

14. Ralph Waldo Emerson, "Greatness" in *The Complete Works of Ralph Waldo Emerson*, vol. 8: *Letters and Social Aims*, Edward Waldo Emerson, ed. (Boston and New York: Houghton, Mifflin and Company, 1903–1904), pp. 301, 308.

15. Title IX refers to a portion of the Education Amendments of 1972. It states in part: "No person in the United States shall, on the basis of sex, be excluded from participation in, be denied the benefits of, or be subjected to discrimination under any education program or activity receiving federal financial assistance."

16. Nichiren, *The Writings*, vol. I, p. 385.

17. Linus Pauling and Daisaku Ikeda, *A Lifelong Quest for Peace* (Boston: Jones and Bartlett Publishers, 1992), p. 67.

Conversation Six
A Return to Self-Reliance

1. Emerson, "Self-Reliance" in *Essays and Lectures*, p. 266.

2. Ibid., p. 271.

3. Every year, beginning in 1983, SGI President Daisaku Ikeda has published a peace proposal on January 26 (the anniversary of the establishing of the Soka Gakkai International in 1975, dubbed "SGI Day") and submitted it to the United Nations. Past proposals are available at the Daisaku Ikeda website: < http://www.daisakuikeda.org. >

4. See Daisaku Ikeda and Hazel Henderson, *Planetary Citizenship* (Santa Monica, Calif.: Middleway Press, 2004), pp. 121, 125.

5. From a dialogue between Daisaku Ikeda and Yehudi Menuhin on April 5, 1992, published in the June 1992 *Seikyo Times*, p. 8.

6. See Eric Hobsbawm, *On the Edge of the New Century* (New York: The New Press, 2000).

7. See Nichiren, *The Writings*, vol. I, p. 513.

8. Ibid., p. 427.

9. Romain Rolland, *Journey Within*, Elsie Pell, trans. (Whitefish, Mont.: Kessinger Publishing, 2004), p. 74.

10. Daisaku Ikeda, "Unforgettable Friends from Around the World," July 2002 *Living Buddhism*, p. 30.

11. Nichiren, *The Writings*, vol. I, p. 536.

CONVERSATION SEVEN
THE RHYTHMS OF NATURE

1. Johann Wolfgang von Goethe, *The Poems of Goethe*, Edgar Alfred Bowring, trans. (London: John W. Parker and Son, West Strand, 1853), p. 114.
2. Henry David Thoreau, *Walden* in *A Week, Walden, The Maine Woods, Cape Cod*, Robert F. Sayre, ed. (New York: The Library of America, 1985), p 569.
3. Ralph Waldo Emerson, *The Heart of Emerson's Journals*, Bliss Perry, ed. (New York: Dover Publications, 1995), p. 4.
4. Ibid., p. 153.
5. Ibid., p. 139.
6. Emerson, *Nature* in *Essays and Lectures*, p. 15.
7. Tsunesaburo Makiguchi, *A Geography of Human Life*, Dayle M. Bethel, trans. (San Francisco: Caddo Gap Press, 2002), p. 62.
8. Luci Tapahonso, "A Blessing" in *A Radiant Curve* (Tucson, Ariz.: University of Arizona Press, 2008), p. 46.
9. Kaneko Ikeda, *Kaneko's Story: A Conversation with Kaneko Ikeda* (Santa Monica: World Tribune Press, 2008), p. 9.
10. Nichiren, *The Writings*, vol. I, p. 313.
11. Ibid., p. 517.
12. F. B. Sanborn, "The Emerson-Thoreau Correspondence: Emerson in Europe" in *The Atlantic Monthly*, June 1892.

CONVERSATION EIGHT
SYMPATHY AND LIKENESS

1. Thoreau, *Walden* in *A Week, Walden, The Maine Woods, Cape Cod*, p. 405.
2. This address was delivered at Cambridge in 1837 before the Harvard Chapter of the Phi Beta Kappa Society, a college fraternity composed of the first twenty-five men in each graduating class. The society met annually, providing a forum for scholars and thinkers considered most distinguished at that time.
3. Makiguchi, *A Geography of Human Life*, p. 21.
4. Soka Book Wave, a Soka University initiative to promote reading among students, received the Japan Association of Private University

Libraries 2011 JAPUL Award in August 2012. Soka Book Wave was launched in 2004 by several on-campus organizations, including the Central Library, student union, and alumni.

5. Simon Ortiz, from the preface to *A Good Journey* in *Woven Stone* (Tucson, Ariz.: University of Arizona Press, 1992), p. 151.

6. *Seikyo Shimbun* is the organizational newspaper published daily (in Japanese) by the Soka Gakkai.

7. Copied for Emerson and given to him by William Allen Wall, the original of the painting hangs in the Pitti Palace and was long believed to have been the work of Michelangelo, but art historians now agree that it was painted by Cecchino Salviati (1610–53). Given the risk of fire, it has been moved to fireproof quarters in the Concord Museum. In the Emerson House, the study is now filled with carefully rendered duplicates.

8. Emerson, "Montaigne; or, the Skeptic" in *Essays and Lectures*, p. 696.

9. Emerson, "Friendship" in *Essays and Lectures*, pp. 348–49.

10. Nichiren, *The Writings*, vol. I, p. 1119.

11. Ibid., p. 502.

CONVERSATION NINE
THE CREATIVE LIFE

1. Georgia O'Keeffe, *Georgia O'Keeffe* (New York: Black Dog and Leventhal Publishers, 1976), words accompanying Plate 17, *New York with Moon*, 1925.

2. Laurie Lisle, *Portrait of an Artist: A Biography of Georgia O'Keeffe* (Albuquerque, N.M.: University of New Mexico Press, 1986), p. 369.

3. Ibid, p. 109.

4. Ibid., p. 167.

5. Emerson, "Art" in *Essays and Lectures*, p. 431.

6. Nichiren, *The Writings*, vol. I, p. 1126. It reads: "The essence of the sutras preached before the Lotus Sutra is that all phenomena arise from the mind. To illustrate, they say that the mind is like the great earth, while the grasses and trees are like all phenomena. But it is not so with the Lotus Sutra. It teaches that the mind itself is the great earth, and that the great earth itself is the grasses and trees."

7. Emerson, "Art" in *Essays and Lectures*, p. 437.

8. Nichiren, *The Writings*, vol. I, p. 1126.

9. Lisle, *Portrait of an Artist*, p. 34.
10. Personal communication.
11. Nichiren, *The Writings*, vol. I, p. 464.
12. Lisle, *Portrait of an Artist*, p. 191.
13. Ibid., p. 209.

CONVERSATION TEN
RENAISSANCE WOMEN

1. Rabindranath Tagore, *The English Writings of Rabindranath Tagore*, vol. 3, Sisir Kumar Das, ed. (New Delhi, India: Sahitya Akademi, 1996), p. 725.
2. Rabindranath Tagore, *The English Writings of Rabindranath Tagore*, vol. 2, Sisir Kumar Das, ed. (New Delhi: Sahitya Akademi, 1996), p. 413.
3. *See* "Walden and Beyond: Awakening East-West Connections" at the website of the Ikeda Center for Peace, Learning, and Dialogue: <http://www.ikedacenter.org/ikeda-forum/2004-walden>.

CONVERSATION ELEVEN
STRENGTH THROUGH CONNECTION

1. Nichiren, *The Writings*, vol. I, p. 923.
2. Emerson, "Heroism" in *Essays and Lectures*, p. 379.
3. Nikolay Yazykov, *Holy Russia and Other Poems*, P. E. Matheson, trans. (London: Oxford University Press, 1918), available online at: <http://www.archive.org/stream/holyrussiaotherpoomathiala/holyrussiaotherpoomathiala_djvu.txt> (accessed on Aug. 22, 2013).
4. Margaret Fuller, *Woman in the Nineteenth Century* (Boston: Greeley & McElrath, 1845), p. 26.
5. From the April 5, 1992, meeting between Yehudi Menuhin and Daisaku Ikeda, published in the June 1992 *Seikyo Times*, p. 8.
6. Nichiren, *The Writings*, vol. I, p. 299.
7. Daisaku Ikeda, "Thoughts on Education for Global Citizenship" in *A New Humanism* (New York: I. B. Tauris, 2010), p. 55.
8. Alex Wayman and Hideko Wayman, trans., *The Lion's Roar of Queen Srimala: A Buddhist Scripture on the Tathagata-garbha Theory* (New York: Columbia University Press, 1974), p. 65.

9. From a meeting between Betty Williams and Daisaku Ikeda on November 6, 2006, reported in the *Soka Gakkai Newsletter* 7035, November 28, 2006.

10. From Daisaku Ikeda's essay series "The Light of the Century of Life" in the *Soka Gakkai Newsletter* 7791, June 9, 2009.

CONVERSATION TWELVE
TO OPEN ALL DOORS

1. Whitman, *Leaves of Grass* in *Poetry and Prose*, p. 383.

2. Ibid., p. 318.

3. Freedom Space: A grassroots initiative launched in 2006 and sponsored by the Organization of Women's Freedom in Iraq, bringing together people of all backgrounds to share their poetry. It started with a single event and became a movement throughout Iraq with monthly and sometimes weekly gatherings. *See* <http://www.huffingtonpost.com/kim-rosen/where-words-melt-walls-th_b_615133.html> (accessed in August 2013).

4. Poets Against the War: Led by poet Sam Hamill, February 12, 2003, became a day of Poetry Against the War conducted as a reading at the White House gates in addition to more than 160 public readings in many different countries and almost all of the 50 states. See <http://poetsagainstthewar.org> (accessed in August 2013).

5. Nichiren, *The Writings of Nichiren Daishonin*, vol. 2 (Tokyo: Soka Gakkai, 2006), p. 861.

6. April 6, 1992, *World Tribune*, p. 5.

7. Walt Whitman, *Specimen Days & Collect [1882–1883]* (New York: Cornell University Library, 2010), p. 149.

8. Walt Whitman, *Notebook and Unpublished Prose Manuscripts*, Edward F. Grier, ed. (New York: New York University Press, 1984), p. 331.

9. Ibid.

10. In Jerome Loving, *Walt Whitman: The Song of Himself* (Berkeley, Calif.: University of California Press, 1999), p. 36.

11. Daisaku Ikeda, *Songs from My Heart*, Burton Watson, trans. (New York: Weatherhill, 1978), p. 73.

12. Translated from Russian. Yeghishe Charents, *Antologicheskii sbornik armyanskoi liriki v dvukx knigakh* (Anthology of Armenian Lyric Poetry) (Yerevan, Armenia: Sovetakan, 1983), p. 214.

13. Whitman, *Leaves of Grass* in *Poetry and Prose*, p. 307.
14. Translated from Japanese. Daisaku Ikeda, "Muchari Shi to Haha" (Oswald Mtshali and His Mother), *Saitama Shimbun*, January 27, 2004.

CONVERSATION THIRTEEN
ROOTED IN DIALOGUE

1. Ralph Waldo Emerson, *Young Emerson Speaks: Unpublished Discourses on Many Subjects*, Arthur Cushman McGiffert, ed. (New York: Kennikat Press, 1968), p. 275.
2. The *Akatsuki* reached Venus on December 7, 2010, but failed to enter orbit. Plans to retry entry into orbit around Venus are being evaluated.
3. This project enables students, teachers, and the public to learn about Earth from the perspective of space. EarthKAM takes photographs of the Earth using a digital camera on the International Space Station by remote control.
4. Richard Norton Smith, *The Harvard Century: The Making of a University to a Nation* (Boston: Harvard University Press, 1998), p. 45.
5. Emerson, "The American Scholar" in *Essays and Lectures*, p. 59.
6. Nichiren, *The Writings*, vol. I, p. 457.
7. Tsunesaburo Makiguchi, *Education for Creative Living* (Ames, Iowa: Iowa State University Press, 1989), p. 289.
8. The dialogue between Daisaku Ikeda and Moscow State University Rector Victor A. Sadovnichy, *Asu no sekai, kyoiku no shimei—nijuisseiki no ningen o kosatsu suru* (tentative translation: The Mission of Education in Tomorrow's World—Thoughts on Humanity in the Twenty-first Century), was published by Ushio Publishing Company in Japanese in April 2013. Rector Sadovnichy and Mr. Ikeda met on several occasions and previously published another dialogue on education that was released as two volumes in Japanese and as one book in Russian.

CONVERSATION FOURTEEN
LEARNING JOURNEYS

1. Translated from Japanese. Tsunesaburo Makiguchi, *Tsunesaburo Makiguchi zenshu*, vol. 8 (Tokyo: Daisan Bunmeisha, 1984), p. 365.

2. "Hsio Kî," or "Record on the Subject of Education," in *Liji*, or *Book of Rites*, James Legge, trans. Available online at: <http://www.sacred-texts.com/cfu/liki2/liki216.htm> (accessed August 2013).

3. Emerson, "The American Scholar" in *Essays and Lectures*, p. 70.

4. Thoreau, *Walden* in *A Week, Walden, The Maine Woods, Cape Cod*, p. 409.

5. Emerson, "The American Scholar" in *Essays and Lectures*, p. 54.

6. José Ortega y Gasset, *Mission of the University* (Piscataway, N.J.: Transaction Publishers, 1991), p. 27.

7. The Soka Education Conference is conducted annually, usually in February, at Soka University of America in Aliso Viejo, Calif. It is typically two or three days of lectures, papers, and workshops organized under the auspices of the Soka Education Student Research Project. *See* <www.sesrp.org> for more information.

8. "Spirit" (the mentality to contribute for the welfare of humankind), "skills" (the attributes required to fulfill such goals), and "service" (utilize the abilities acquired through one's studies for the benefit of others, and cultivate the mentality, leadership, and courage needed to pursue such actions).

Conversation Fifteen
The Solidest Thing

1. William Wordsworth, *William Wordsworth: The Major Works*, Stephen Gill, ed. (New York: Oxford University Press, 2000) p. 200.

2. Emerson, "Friendship" in *Essays and Lectures*, p. 351.

3. Ibid., p. 346.

4. André Suarès was one of the pseudonyms used by Félix-André-Yves Scantrel, a French poet and critic. From 1912 onward, he was one of the four "pillars" of the Nouvelle Revue Française, along with André Gide, Paul Claudel, and Paul Valéry.

5. William Wordsworth, *The Prelude: Or Growth of a Poet's Mind* (Oxford: Clarendon Press, 1926), p. 80.

6. Emerson, "Friendship" in *Essays and Lectures*, p. 350.

7. Daisaku Ikeda and Victor A. Sadovnichy, *Gaku wa hikari* (The Illuminating Power of Learning) and *Atarashiki jinrui o, atarashiki sekai o* (Beyond the Century: Dialogue on Education and Society).

8. Boulding and Ikeda, *Into Full Flower*, p. 95.

9. Emerson, "Each and All" in *Essays and Poems*, Joel Porte, Harold Bloom, and Paul Kane, eds. (New York: The Library of America, 1883), p. 1059.

10. Boulding and Ikeda, *Into Full Flower*, p. 95.

CONVERSATION SIXTEEN
INFINITE POWER INSIDE

1. Horace Traubel, *With Walt Whitman in Camden*, vol. 1 (New York: Mitchell Kennerley, 1915), p. 69.

2. Emerson, "The Method of Nature" in *Essays and Lectures*, p. 123.

3. Emerson, *Representative Men* in *Essays and Lectures*, p. 630.

4. Ibid., p. 646.

5. Emerson, "The Divinity School Address" in *Essays and Lectures*, p. 79.

6. Emerson, *Representative Men* in *Essays and Lectures*, p. 617.

7. Daisaku Ikeda conducted a dialogue with two past presidents of the John Dewey Society, Dr. Jim Garrison and Dr. Larry Hickman, who is also director of the Center for Dewey Studies. The publication is tentatively titled *New Currents in Humane Education: Dewey and Value-Creating Pedagogy*.

8. Emerson, "Education" in *Complete Works*, vol. 10, p. 149.

9. "Good" is that which enhances the life of an entire community or society; "gain" refers to all that concretely enhances the entirety of an individual's existence; and "beauty" is esthetic value that enhances specific aspects of the individual's life. Here value does not point to something abstract or disembodied, but to the positive transformation of our actual experience of life.

10. Emerson, "Education" in *Complete Works*, vol. 10, p. 135.

11. Emerson, "Friendship" in *Essays and Lectures*, p. 339.

Index

About the Authors

SARAH WIDER is Professor of English and Women's Studies at Colgate University, where she specializes in the American Renaissance, American women writers of the late nineteenth and early twentieth centuries, and Native American literature. Dr. Wider is former president of the Ralph Waldo Emerson Society, and her publications include *The Critical Reception of Emerson: Unsettling All Things* and *Anna Tilden: Unitarian Culture and the Problem of Self-Representation.*

DAISAKU IKEDA is President of the Soka Gakkai International, a lay Buddhist organization with more than twelve million members worldwide. He has written and lectured widely on Buddhism, humanism, and global ethics. More than fifty of his dialogues have been published, including conversations with figures such as Elise Boulding, Vincent Harding, Mikhail Gorbachev, Hazel Henderson, Joseph Rotblat, Linus Pauling, and Arnold Toynbee. Dedicated to education promoting humanistic ideals, in 1971 President Ikeda founded Soka University in Tokyo and, in 2001, Soka University of America in Aliso Viejo, California.

The front cover image is a detail from: Pieced Quilt. 1930.
Made by Y. L. Amish, Indiana. Wool and cotton, 84 x 71 in.